PRICE 6D.

ALDERSHOT & DISTRICT TRACTION CO LTD

FARNHAM LONDON EXPRESS SERVICE

OFFICIAL TIME TABLE

4th OCTOBER 1954 to 22nd MAY 1955

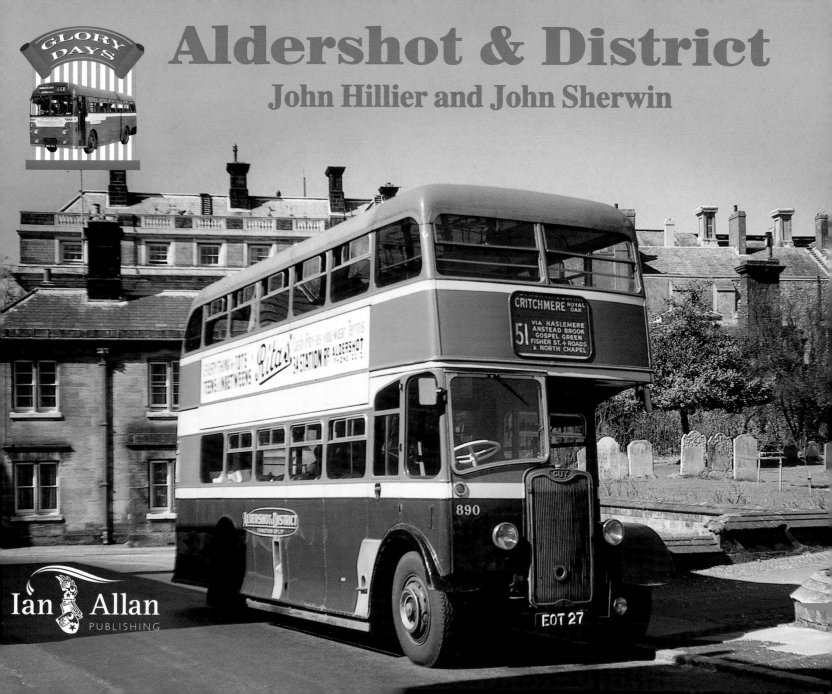

Aldershot & District
John Hillier and John Sherwin

GLORY DAYS

CRITCHMERE ROYAL OAK

51 VIA HASLEMERE
ANSTEAD BROOK
GOSPEL GREEN
FISHER ST. 4 ROADS
& NORTH CHAPEL

890

GUY

ALDERSHOT DISTRICT

EOT 27

Ian Allan PUBLISHING

Contents

Front cover:
Recently outshopped Dennis Loline 363 (SOU 471) awaits departure from Farnham Road bus station at Guildford in April 1968. The bus station, toilet block and telephone boxes have since been cleared, and the site is currently a car park. *Brian Oxborough*

Back cover:
The Wharf car park in Godalming was the terminus for services 45 from Farnham and 60 from Dunsfold, and the adjacent café was well used by bus crews. Seen on service 60 in November 1966, 235 (LOU 63) was the first of the 1954 batch of Dennis Falcon P5s with 30-seat Strachans bodywork. The introduction of these one-man-operated buses, with lightweight bodywork, single rear wheels and a five-speed gearbox, reduced operating costs and saved many marginal rural routes. This particular vehicle was withdrawn two months after the photograph was taken. *Brian Oxborough*

First published 2004

ISBN 0 7110 2956 3

Published by Ian Allan Publishing

an imprint of Ian Allan Publishing Ltd, Hersham, Surrey KT12 4RG.

Printed by Ian Allan Printing Ltd, Hersham, Surrey KT12 4RG.

Code: 0404/B1

Title page:
Petworth House forms the backdrop to Guy Arab II 890 (EOT 27) just days before the latter's withdrawal in March 1965. Its 8ft-wide body, dating from May 1954, was fitted onto a 7ft 6in chassis dating from 1945. It was on an enthusiasts' tour of the route of service 51 (Critchmere–Haslemere–Petworth), which was last operated with double-deckers on 30 March 1958. *Les Smith*

Endpapers:
For publicity purposes the company produced a number of attractively coloured illustrations for use as timetable covers and official calendars. The artwork was prepared by over-painting monochrome originals. These examples show a Dennis Lancet J3 crossing Tilford Bridge, the first of the company's AEC Reliance coaches at Aldershot's Wellington Monument, another 1954 Reliance coach passing Godalming 'Pepper Pot' and a Dennis Loline in East Street, Farnham.

This book has been compiled by members of the Aldershot & District Bus Interest Group

Authors:
John Hillier and John Sherwin
Photographic Collectors:
Tony Wright and Les Smith
Caption Authors:
Peter Trevaskis and Tony Wright
Caption Editor: Phil Jacob
Co-ordinating Editor:
Peter Holmes

Introduction

For us the 'glory days' of the Aldershot & District Traction Company Limited, often abbreviated to 'Tracco' and sometimes humorously referred to as 'Have a shot and risk it' by our families, were from the World War 2 era to the demise of the company in December 1971. Unashamedly, we have based the majority of our work for this book on personal recollections of the heydays of the Forties, Fifties and Sixties and research into the company (A&D) during this time-frame.

To set the scene, we need to explore the humble beginnings of the flourishing bus company as we knew it. The first public-transport journeys between Aldershot and Farnborough were made nearly a century ago, in 1906. With special permission, 'The Aldershot & Farnborough Motor Omnibus Company Limited' ran half-hourly services on the shortest route between Aldershot and Farnborough, which was through the military camp. It purchased second-hand 20hp Milnes-Daimler double-deckers with 28 seats. Despite its growth during the first few years, the company needed new capital for re-equipment and expansion. An offer was made by the British Automobile Traction Co Ltd in 1912 to finance and enter partnership with the Aldershot & Farnborough company. The Board of the company accepted the offer and, with a new name, the 'Tracco' was born on 24 July 1912.

The newly formed company started to expand, with services to Camberley and Farnham. It purchased from the London & South Western Railway a service of buses running from Farnham to Haslemere through Hindhead and entered into an agreement with the railway company by providing luxury vehicles with curtains and fittings for First-class passengers. Early in 1914 a service from Aldershot to Guildford was established. World War 1 meant that thousands of extra troops were based in Aldershot, the 'Home of the British Army'. When off-duty, these troops in training needed to move around and outside the camp,

to local shops and the station. These were troubled times for the company, which was short of skilled men. By 1916 many had been enlisted for military service and only two fitters and some apprentices were available to look after 42 buses, 22 petrol lorries, 12 steam wagons, six parcel vans and four cars.

After the war the company grew rapidly and even tried its hand at coach body building. In the 1920s and '30s expansion was evident. Service 1, from Aldershot to Egham, started in 1921, and Guildford–Horsham route 33 was introduced in 1923. By 1927 the fleet had grown to 140 buses operating 43 routes, and in the following year the first covered-top double-decker was purchased for local use. The 'bus wars' of the Twenties led to the 1930 Road Traffic Act, which regulated passenger services. A&D must have been delighted when this came into force, because the fierce competition with rival companies had made its losses in 1928/9 quite worrying for shareholders, who received no dividend. The Act set up Traffic Commissioners, who took control of the licensing of services. The company soon

▲ The formation of the Aldershot & District Traction Co Ltd in 1912 was followed by the introduction of new vehicles. Seven of these 34-seat Leyland S double-deckers enabled the new concern to open up several new routes in and around Aldershot. Their bodies were built by a boatbuilding subsidiary of the new owner, the British Electric Traction Co, called the Immisch Launch & Boat Co. *Peter Holmes collection*

Aldershot & District always included a clear route map in its timetables (except in wartime). This version dates from the late 1950s.

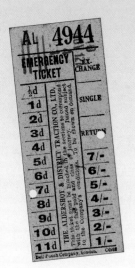

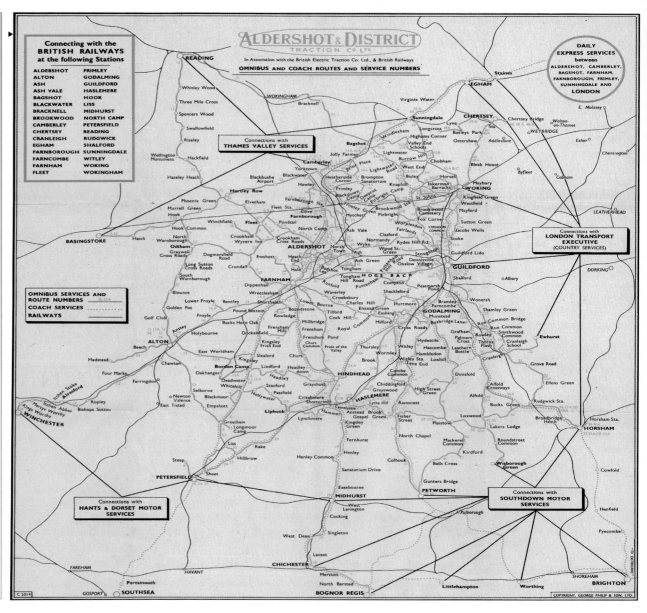

recovered, and by 1930 the fleet had grown to 236 Dennis vehicles. Three years later the London Passenger Transport Board was created. The Act which saw this change also drew up statutory (instead of negotiated) boundaries between companies. As a result, the company lost three routes east of Guildford to places such as Dorking, Ewhurst and Merrow.

Many interesting stories about the company are on record, showing the human angle, such as this one from the Golden Jubilee booklet produced by A&D in 1962 to celebrate 'Fifty Years of Public Service':

'During the 30s the Company transported many thousands of visitors to the famous Aldershot Tattoo at Rushmoor Arena from railway stations in the district. The nerve centre of the organisation on these June nights was at Badajos Barracks Square, where Army field telephones were used by Mr. Gray, the Traffic Manager, and his staff to regulate the bus traffic.'

With the advent of the Farnborough Air Show in 1948, the skills and knowledge gained by moving so many people to and from the tattoo before the war came in useful again. Special bus services were required between Aldershot railway station and the Air Show site at Farnborough. In 1953, for example, a bus left Aldershot for the show every 30 seconds, and over 80,000 passengers were carried over the three days of the show.

In the same booklet the ups and downs of the company are revealed by a comparison of passenger numbers at the turn of each decade. The peak year for travel was 1950, when 52 million passengers were carried by the company. This compares with 18 million in 1930, around 25 million in 1940 and just about 46 million in 1960. World War 2 brought about some very tough economies with fuel rationing and restrictions of movement. The company survived by making cuts to services, eight of which were never revived after hostilities ceased. Apart from this, some of the single-decker buses were commandeered for use as ambulances and by the military. The relaxation of these measures happened in the second half of 1944. It was not long

before A&D was developing and reaching agreements in Guildford with a local independent firm — Yellow Bus Services — to co-ordinate services with joint operation.

The business started to expand again with the reinstatement of coastal and London coach services in 1946. During this early-postwar period, when few families had a car and people relied on public transport for travel to and from work, the shops and the cinema, A&D was ready to respond. Buses converted for wartime uses returned to service, and, until the increase in car ownership made bus and coach travel seem less attractive, the company continued to expand. How fondly we recall the era of quieter roads and full buses! In this book, memories of these 'glory days' are brought to life with the aid of personal recollections and contemporary photographs.

John Hillier
John Sherwin
August 2003

▲ The entire intake of new vehicles during 1929 was of Dennis manufacture. OU 1806, a Dennis EV, had a 32-seat Strachans body with rear entrance, which layout remained standard for A&D until the 1950s. This scene was recorded at Aldershot bus station. *Mike Stephens collection*

1. Supporting Dennis

Dennis Lancet AOT 602, dating from 1936, in Ridgway Road, Farnham, operating on service 10A (Farnham–Rowledge). This Lancet was one of the many that served as ambulances during World War 2. When they were returned to service in 1944-6, they had their petrol engines replaced with Dennis O4 oil engines. However, unlike most of its fellows, AOT 602 was not rebodied to prolong its life and was withdrawn in 1949, five years earlier than the majority of the batch.
Douglas Hawkins

Pictured outside Hindhead garage on 1 May 1954, Dennis Lancet 666 (AOT 599) was new in 1936 with a petrol engine and 32-seat Strachans body. Three years after returning from wartime ambulance duties, in 1946, it was fitted with an oil engine and a new body supplied by Vincent's of Reading.
John Gillham

To our generation, born in the late 1930s and 1940s, the names 'Aldershot & District' and 'Dennis' were synonymous, because we lived in A&D's operating area and depended on its Dennis single- and double-deck buses for our everyday transport. As a result we developed an affection for both companies. The relationship had started in 1914 when A&D took over Guildford & District Motor Services, which had operated locally built Dennis buses, and during the long association A&D had often assisted Dennis in the development of prototype buses. From 1924 until the heyday of A&D in the 1950s, Dennis was the primary supplier. In the early 1950s the total fleet comprised 341 buses and coaches, of which 95% were Dennis. Although it ceased to purchase Dennis single-deckers in 1956, the company remained loyal for the supply of double-deckers until 1971, when A&D merged with the Thames Valley Traction Co to form the Thames Valley & Aldershot Omnibus Co, better known by its trading name of Alder Valley.

Our association with A&D began in early childhood during World War 2 and the early-postwar period, travelling on Dennis Lancet I former coaches (1932 batch: CG 1317-28; 1934 batch: CG 6357/8; 1935 batch: CG 9596-9603/5) and single-deck buses (1936 batch: AOT 587-605 and BAA 387-96) fitted initially with the Dennis Big Four 5.6-litre petrol engine but later provided with diesel engines. All had Strachans half-cab, rear-entrance, 32-seat bodywork and luxurious interior trim. The more stylish Lancet II buses were introduced in 1937 (1937 batch: BOT 288-307; 1938 batch: COR 164-91) and the coaches in 1938 (COR 151-63); both types were fitted with the Dennis O4 diesel engine and represented the first diesel-powered single-deck vehicles in the fleet. The later Lancet II single-deck buses delivered in 1939 (DHO 267-305) and 1941 (ECG 380/1, 424) were fitted with the Gardner 5LW diesel. The half-cab, rear-entrance, 32-seat bodywork was produced by Strachans and also by Dennis, the design becoming the standard for A&D until the early 1950s. After the war A&D undertook a programme to rebody most of the 1936 batch of Lancet I buses with the new-style bodywork produced by Strachans or Vincent of Reading and at the same time fitted the Dennis O4 diesel engine. The 1941 batch of Lancet II buses were also renovated after the war by Portsmouth Aviation.

The arrival in 1945 of the prototype Lancet J3 (EOR 743)
heralded the introduction of the Dennis O6 diesel engine and
the Dennis five-speed gearbox. This driveline combination was
used on all subsequent Lancet buses and coaches and afforded a
reduction in noise and a smoother ride. Unlike the production
Lancet J3 buses which followed in 1947 (1947 batch:
EOU 435-74; 1948 batch: EOU 475-84, GAA 580-600;
1949 batch: GAA 601-8 and GOU 801-23) and the coaches in
1948 (GAA 609-23), all of which were fitted with standard 32-
seat single-deck bodywork by Strachans, the prototype was
fitted with a unique Dennis-built body with lower floor and
waistline. The Lancet J10s (HOU 899, 901-11) entered A&D
service in 1950, again with Strachans half-cab rear-entrance
bodywork, but now with 38 seats. This was our first experience
of travelling on the new regulation 8ft-wide, 30ft-long bus.
They seemed huge when compared with previous single-deck
buses and were fitted with a white steering wheel to remind the
driver of the width — a feature of all subsequent 8ft-wide A&D
vehicles. We always had great sympathy for the driver, isolated
in the half cab, exposed to the elements, because with no cab
heater and plenty of draughts he was cold in the winter and very

Dennis Lance J3 962 (GAA 598) stands at the eastern terminus of service 45 (Farnham–Godalming) at the Wharf car park in Godalming. The service was introduced by May's of Elstead and taken over by A&D in January 1928. No 962 was one of 102 virtually identical buses, with 32-seat Strachans bodywork, delivered between December 1946 and March 1949, of which the last survivors remained in service until 1961. *Peter Trevaskis*

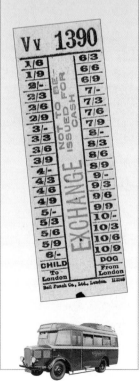

hot in summer heat. These 12 buses were always nicknamed 'Brabs', since, like the contemporary Bristol Brabazon airliner, they were so much bigger than anything we had seen before.

Insufficient seating capacity in the late 1940s resulted in many passengers' having to stand on fully loaded buses, and better utilisation of single-deck interior space became an issue for the bus industry. The initial response from A&D came in 1951 with the Dennis Dominant (HOU 900), a prototype single-decker with a horizontally mounted underfloor Dennis O6 engine and Hobbs automatic gearbox. Improved utilisation of interior space afforded by the new width and length regulations was obtained with a radical new centre-entrance Strachans body design, with the seating capacity increased to 41 from the previous norm of 32. Even as youngsters we appreciated the significant step forward in technology — and the opportunity to sit at the front, next to the driver! However, the gearbox proved unreliable and

required replacement with the less-smooth gear change of the conventional five-speed crash-type 'box. Things were not going well for Dennis and the Dominant when, in 1953, additional service trials were undertaken with non-Dennis underfloor-engined single-deck chassis. It was hoped that the loan of the Dennis Lancet UF (KOT 600) would prove successful, but sadly the results of the nine months' evaluation proved unsatisfactory, and Dennis ceased to be a contender for supplying A&D's next generation of single-deck buses and coaches.

By 1953 the traditional half-cab with exposed radiator had become unfashionable, and, having not yet selected the underfloor-engined chassis to form the basis of its next generation of single-deck buses, A&D took delivery of 15 Lancet J10C coaches (LAA 223-37) as an interim measure. These were essentially J10s with Strachans full-fronted 38-seat bodywork on conventional front-engined chassis. They had an

Against the familiar backdrop of Gale & Polden's print works and the Hippodrome Theatre, Strachans-bodied Dennis Lancet J10 183 (HOU 909) occupies the spare bay at Aldershot bus station during layover on 15 March 1958. The J10s were the first buses in the A&D fleet to the new 30ft-long, 8ft-wide dimensions and were each fitted with a white steering wheel as a reminder to drivers. They seated 38 and were the first single-deckers for many years, apart from the Falcons, not to be supplied with 'band boxes'. They were powered by Dennis O6 engines with a five-speed crash gearbox. *Tony Wright*

No 174 (HOU 900), the prototype Dennis Dominant supplied to A&D in May 1951, waits in Aldershot bus station on 21 March 1959. Its unusual Strachans body seated 41 and had a central entrance positioned just forward of the rear wheels; the emergency exit was behind the driver's door, on the offside. Among the Dominant's drawbacks was the relatively high fuel consumption, Dennis building only one other such chassis, but HOU 900 nevertheless served for 14 years with the 'Tracco'. *Tony Wright*

Small, short-wheelbase buses were essential for use on the deeply rural routes of Hampshire and Surrey. The Dennis Ace made its debut in 1934, and over the next 12 months A&D took delivery of 24 to replace the Dennis G and similar types. The first batch, represented by brand-new CG 6392, had 20-seat Strachans bodies, while the remainder received bodywork (by Strachans or E. D. Abbott of Farnham) removed from unsuccessful Morris RP vehicles. Because of the snout-like appearance of the bonnet, the Ace became widely known as the 'Flying Pig'. *John Aldridge collection*

A 24-seat all-Dennis Falcon P3 new in 1950 with 20 seats, 157 (GOU 857) stands awaiting its next duty on the approach to Hindhead garage in September 1958. Hindhead normally used this type on the 13 group of services from Haslemere as well as on the 17 from Grayshott to Farnham and Ewshot. They were superseded by the larger Falcon P5 when withdrawn in the early 1960s. The little buses on service 17 were known locally as 'Whippets' — a name which was continued until the service ceased. *Tony Wright*

10

unusual appearance, which probably resulted from the combination of a modern-style coach front and a traditional rear-entrance body. The J10Cs were the last full-sized Dennis single-deckers purchased by A&D and continued in service until 1963.

Many of A&D's deeply rural bus routes were along narrow country lanes where the Dennis Ace and subsequently the Dennis Falcon P3 and P5 provided short-wheelbase, normal-control, extremely manœuvrable buses. Introduced in 1934, the Ace (1934 batch: CG 6391-6405, 9010-3; 1935 batch: CG 9014-9; 1936 batch: AOT 581-6) pre-dated the modern OMO midibus. With Strachans or Abbott 20-seat bodywork it was probably the cutest vehicle ever operated by A&D, and, because the bonnet resembled the snout of a pig, it was widely referred to as the 'Flying Pig'. To our delight, the tradition of the small, friendly rural bus continued with the arrival in 1939 of the Falcon P3 (DHO 266, DOT 470-7). They were fitted with Strachans 20-seat bodywork and powered by a Dennis 3.77-litre petrol engine; postwar models used the Gardner 4LK diesel engine and Dennis bodywork (1949 batch: GOU 848-52; 1950 batch: GOU 853-62). Further changes in legislation during the early 1950s permitted one-man operation of buses of higher seating capacity, and in 1954 the Dennis Falcon P5 (1954 batch: LOU 63-77; 1956 batch: POR 421-8), developed in conjunction with A&D, entered service. However, excessive engine noise pervaded the all-aluminium 30-seat Strachans body, and it was given the nickname 'conker box'. Most passengers were not too disappointed when, 13 years later, they were withdrawn from service.

Successive forms of Dennis Lance and, latterly, Loline provided the primary mode of travel by double-decker from 1936 until 1971. The first two Lance chassis, introduced to A&D in 1936, were prototypes and used different types of engine. One (AOT 580) was fitted with the unsuccessful Lanova diesel engine; this chassis was dismantled in 1937, reconstructed with a Dennis O4 diesel engine and re-registered (CCG 188). The other (BAA 386) was fitted with a Gardner 5LW diesel engine. Both incorporated the new-style radiator and a more modern design of 48-seat, low-height Strachans bodywork, although the original all-steel bodywork on AOT 580 (later CCG 188) was replaced with a conventionally constructed Strachans body in 1941. However, the Lance II, which entered A&D service in 1937 (CCG 311-51) used the Dennis O4 diesel engine, the Dennis five-speed gearbox and the same new-style radiator as fitted to the new Lance and Lancet II — a feature which showed that the new generation of buses were from the same family. The engine in

The arrival of a production batch of 41 Dennis Lance IIs during 1937 resulted in the complete elimination of A&D's previous double-deck fleet. All had 48-seat 'lowbridge' Strachans bodywork and Dennis O4 oil engines. CCG 342 is about to climb Queen's Road, Aldershot, with the prospect of more severe gradients ahead *en route* to Upper Hale. Despite what is shown on the blind, the ultimate destination was Farnham. This was not regarded as a direct Aldershot–Farnham route, and a higher fare was originally demanded for the full journey. This bus was never rebodied and was withdrawn in 1950, while its rebodied companions lasted another eight years. *Douglas Hawkins*

This April 1949 photograph of the lower saloon of the East Lancs body fitted to the 1937 Dennis Lance chassis of CCG 311 in 1945 shows clearly the intrusion of the sunken gangway on the offside, necessary to permit access to the upper-deck seating on lowbridge buses. The unprotected lamp bulbs are also clearly visible, as is the lack of any form of bulkhead heater for the comfort of the passengers. Alternate half-drop windows were fitted to both decks to provide ventilation.
Maurice C. Lawson

Dennis Lance II 729 (CCG 326) waits at Aldershot bus station to depart on route 15 to Upper Hale Schools on 18 January 1954. Its original 48-seat Strachans body of 1937 was replaced in 1946 by the 48-seat East Lancs body of prewar design seen here. At this time football pools were very much in vogue, as is apparent from the Vernon's advert carried between the decks.
Tony Wright

Dennis Lance K4 207 (LOU 35) stands outside the Southern Region station at Reading prior to setting out southbound to Aldershot on service 12. When new in January 1954 this vehicle appeared with light green below the waistline but a dark-green radiator grille; the next K4 (208) was the first to be painted dark green below the waistline. The first 20 K4s had East Lancs bodies.
Alistair Douglas / Photobus

No 229 (LOU 57), a 'lightweight' Dennis Lance K4 with 56-seat Weymann body similar to the 1954 'Orion' design, stands at Reading Stations before setting out on service 12. These vehicles did not give as comfortable a ride as did the heavier East Lancs-bodied versions and were soon taken off the long-distance services, being relegated to local operations in the Aldershot and Guildford areas.
Geoffrey Morant

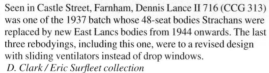

Seen in Castle Street, Farnham, Dennis Lance II 716 (CCG 313) was one of the 1937 batch whose 48-seat bodies Strachans were replaced by new East Lancs bodies from 1944 onwards. The last three rebodyings, including this one, were to a revised design with sliding ventilators instead of drop windows.
D. Clark / Eric Surfleet collection

CCG 319 was subsequently replaced by a Gardner 5LW type in 1943. The Lance II models which arrived in 1940 (DOT 478-83), were fitted with the Gardner 5LW engine and Strachans bodywork based on a teak frame, presumably for improved durability.

By 1944 the bodywork of the earlier Lances was suffering the effects of wear and tear. Fortunately renovation was not subject to wartime utility regulations, and as a result, between 1944 and 1948, 22 of the 1937 Lance IIs, plus BAA 386, had their Strachans bodies replaced with 48-seat bodywork by East Lancs, the Dennis O4 engine being replaced with the Gardner 5LW on one Lance (BAA 386) and most Lance IIs. For most, the bodywork was to the East Lancs prewar design, although the postwar design was used for the last three vehicles (CCG 313/4/30) in 1948. This enabled us to travel in improved comfort until the Lances were withdrawn in 1958. Although we didn't appreciate it at the time, it was probable that this renovation programme represented the demise of Strachans double-deck bodywork for A&D and the commencement of what was to become a long-standing relationship between A&D and East Lancs. This resulted in East Lancs' providing the bodywork for the forthcoming Lance K3s, most of the Lance K4s and all of the Loline type in 1958.

There was considerable similarity in appearance between the postwar East Lancs bodywork used on the renovated Lances and that on the new 51-seat Lance K3s, built to the latest postwar standards, which entered service in 1949/50 (GAA 624-9, GOU 824-47 and HOT 692-701). However, one noticeable external difference was the attractive new-style alloy radiator. The Lance K3, fitted with the Dennis O6 engine and five-speed gearbox, provided new levels of comfort, especially with the presence of a heater in the lower saloon. For many, the Lance K3 double-decker represented the ultimate postwar Dennis conventional rear-open-platform design.

With the introduction in 1954 of the 8ft-wide, 27ft-long Lance K4, A&D reverted to the Gardner 5LW engine using new or reconditioned units combined with the five-speed gearbox. The flowing lines of the 56-seat East Lancs bodywork graced most of the K4s (LOU 31-50); the alternative 56-seat Weymann 'Orion' lightweight alloy bodywork was fitted to 12 of the batch (LOU 51-62), although this appeared less robust. However, Dennis's new-look 'tin-front' grille, which concealed the radiator on both designs of bodywork, was considered to be rather ugly.

By the mid-1950s, with A&D sourcing its new fleet of single-deck vehicles from elsewhere, the relationship with Dennis had

Dennis Lance K3 142 (GOU 842) of 1950 is seen in pristine condition in its early days at the terminus of service 8A (Aldershot–Fleet via Kings Road) in Albert Street, Fleet. These buses had 51 seats.
David Sharwood

deteriorated, and it appeared that the Falcon P5 might be the last type that Dennis would supply. However, in 1956 Dennis was granted a licence to build variants of the Bristol Lodekka, (available only to State-owned operators) as the Loline. In 1958 no fewer than 34 of these (SOU 444-77) entered service with A&D as the company's first 8ft-wide, 30ft-long, 68-seat double-deckers, these having an enclosed rear entrance with an electrically operated sliding door. This was also the first time A&D had used the Gardner 6LW engine and a new Dennis five-speed gearbox, and we immediately noticed the smoothness of the Gardner six-cylinder engine when compared with the earlier five-cylinder unit used in the Lance K4. The drop-centre rear axle was a brilliant design, because it enabled low-level access to the lower saloon while maintaining a low overall height without recourse to a sunken gangway. As a result the Loline could have a central gangway in the upper saloon — a new experience for A&D passengers brought up on buses with a sunken side gangway. No longer would there be 'Please lower head when leaving seat' notices

on the back of the offside seats in the lower saloon — a characteristic of all previous A&D double-deckers.

To improve safety and comfort, in 1961 A&D introduced the front-entrance Dennis Loline III, which incorporated the Gardner 6LW engine, Dennis five-speed gearbox and air suspension of the rear axle. East Lancs was unable to meet A&D delivery dates, so Alexander and Weymann were contracted to supply the low-height, centre-gangway, 68-seat bodywork, with air-operated door. The concept was the same for both designs, although the two bodybuilders employed very different styling. For a conventional front-engined double-decker we preferred the Weymann bodywork (1964 batch: 481-502 KOT; 1965 batch: AAA 503-30C) because it was less bulbous than the whale-like Alexander (1961 batch: 394-413 COR; 1962 batch: 121-40 DOR). During 1962 Dennis decided to abandon bus manufacture, but as a result of demands from operators the decision was rescinded, and manufacture of the Loline III for A&D resumed. The type continued in service until 1980 with Alder Valley.

Guildford's traffic pattern changed frequently in the late Sixties and early Seventies, leading to numerous alterations in A&D's routeings. Here 409 (409 COR), an Alexander-bodied Loline III on service 20C, sets out eastwards on what amounted to a circular tour of the lower part of the town (crossing the river twice!), before reaching Woodbridge Road for its northbound journey.
Arnold Richardson / Photobus

The second batch of Alexander-bodied ▶▶ Loline IIIs, arriving in 1962, had illuminated offside advertisement panels, which were not all utilised, no doubt because of the greater cost to the advertiser. Conventional advertisements were often applied on top of these panels. No 433 (125 DOR) waits at Farnham Road bus station, Guildford, for departure on service 23.
Geoffrey Morant

Not long after delivery in 1965, the Dennis Loline IIIs with Weymann bodywork replaced the rear-entrance Lolines which had operated service 14 (Aldershot–Winchester) since they were new in 1958. No 520 (AAA 520C) prepares to leave Winchester's Hants & Dorset bus station on a short to Alresford. This bus was originally registered as 520 KOT, but Hampshire started using its year-suffix registrations on 1 January 1965 and the number was changed.
Arnold Richardson / Photobus

2. Forced Change

During World War 2 Dennis ceased manufacture of all civilian buses and lorries as production switched to military vehicles, tracked personnel carriers and Churchill tanks. A delayed batch of Lancet II single-deckers with Strachans utility bodywork and fitted with the Gardner 5LW diesel engine (ECG 600, ECG 851/2, ECG 945, EHO 162) was delivered in 1942, but until early 1945 — just before the end of the war — no new Dennis bus entered the A&D fleet. For the first time in recent history Dennis had not been the primary supplier to A&D.

To bridge the initial gap, two Leyland Titan TD7s (ECG 943/4) — 48-seat low-height double-deck buses with metal-framed East Lancs bodywork and sunken gangway in the upper saloon — were introduced in 1942. The TD7 was a new experience, as it was the first occasion since 1912 that A&D had purchased Leyland vehicles, and was an event never to be repeated in the history of the company. The bodywork was to prewar specification and marked the start of the A&D relationship with East Lancs, which lasted until the late 1950s.

Government restriction on new bus construction was relaxed during 1942, with four manufacturers nominated for production. The Guy Arab Mk I was the only double-deck chassis readily available at the time, so in 1942 A&D introduced its first examples (1942 batch: EHO 173, 217/86, 316; 1943 batch: EHO 508/87, 695), powered by the 7.0-litre, Gardner 5LW engine driving through a four-speed gearbox. The 48-seat Strachans wartime-specification utility bodywork was extremely basic, with a very angular, box-like appearance and drop windows with no winding mechanism. The first sighting of the spartan utility Arab, together with the distinctive smell of the newly painted interior can instantly be recalled 60 years later. The roof was of single-skin metal, riveted on the interior to the numerous cross-braces and painted a wishy-washy 'off white' colour. The rear emergency exit in the upper rear panel was blank, with no window, so people often missed the bus because they were not visible to the conductor when he or she was upstairs. Destination boxes, at the front and side only, comprised a single panel but still displayed destination, including towns and villages *en route*. Clearly, A&D felt no need to conceal the

In wartime guise, ECG 943, one of the two Leyland TD7s bought in 1942 with 48-seat East Lancs bodywork, is seen in Reading on the busy trunk service 12 from Aldershot. The basic timetable (not accounting for duplication) required two vehicles, and the Leylands were allocated to this service for a number of years. *W. J. Haynes / Southdown Enthusiasts' Club*

A 'utility' Guy Arab, EHO 587, of 1943 vintage parked in the 'spare' bay of Aldershot bus station, some time after the end of World War 2. Note the interesting blind display for service 3C These early A&D Guys had bodies built by Strachans. *Tony Wright collection*

names of the localities from any enemy travelling within the Aldershot area, although the general public and local authorities were often over-zealous in this respect; the close proximity of the Royal Aircraft Establishment at Farnborough and of other military installations created a fear of infiltration by spies or German parachutists. The worst feature of these buses was the austere upholstered seating, which was very uncomfortable during long journeys.

Further relaxation of restrictions allowed some improvement in Strachans' body styling, reflected in the Guy Arab Mk IIs (EHO 806/18, EHO 952/83, EOR 28, 288) which arrived in 1943/4. The reinstated windows in the rear emergency exit were welcomed and resulted in fewer people missing the bus. However, comfort had taken a further down-turn with the introduction of the dreaded 'button catcher' — the honey-coloured, varnished, slatted wooden seat, apparently adopted to enable semi-skilled and/or unskilled labour to construct the bodywork. As the war proceeded restrictions on deliveries of new buses were relaxed.

However, in 1944 there was a minor setback in styling with the arrival of a few Mk IIs fitted with Roe bodywork (EOR 29-31, 373) which looked even more austere than the first Strachans utility bodywork. However, things did improve in early 1945 with the arrival of Mk IIs with Weymann prototype metal-framed bodywork (EOR 374-6) and a return to some semblance of styling. The windows, still without winding mechanism, had rounded lower corners, the roof domes were nicely rounded, and the traditional two-part destination box reappeared at the front and on the side. The final batch of Mk IIs also arrived in 1945, with Strachans semi-utility bodywork (EOT 25-30) and a return to a more shapely rear dome. There was no change in the overall frontal appearance, but boarding the correct bus was greatly assisted by the two-part destination box at the front, rear and side. Having boarded the correct bus, we were greatly relieved at the sight and feel of comfortable, upholstered seats manufactured to peacetime standards.

At the end of the war A&D had a fleet of seven Mk Is and 19 Mk IIs. They were operated over the most heavily loaded short-distance routes until the late 1940s, when the utility bodies displayed a sad and outdated appearance. The effect of wear and tear, the use of unseasoned wood for the framework, poor-quality materials and the adoption of less-exacting quality standards had at last taken their toll. The only characteristic of the Arabs which cheered us during those drab days of the late 1940s was the advertising panels displayed on either side of the front destination box, along the upper side panels and on the upper rear corners and lower rear panel.

In 1950 there was a marked improvement in style and comfort with the rebodying of Mk I and earlier Mk II Arab chassis with 51-seat, Weymann bodywork. These were followed in 1954 by further Mk IIs (EOT 25-30) rebodied with 56-seat, East Lancs bodywork similar to that used on the Dennis Lance K4 introduced in 1954. To us the most interesting and unusual aspect was the combination of 8ft-wide, 27ft-long body and 7ft 6in-wide, 26ft-long chassis. Aesthetically, the overhang on each side appeared to indicate incorrect body-width: track ratio, suggesting poor driveability and instability. But the appearance proved deceptive: the buses were a success, with no undue rocking or rolling in the aisle when negotiating sharp corners.

No information survives to confirm why A&D retained the Guy Arabs; with hindsight we can only speculate that the combination of sturdy chassis and Gardner engine made for a cost-effective double-deck bus. In 1953, meanwhile, the company purchased a Guy Arab LUF (KOT 113), powered with a horizontally-mounted underfloor Gardner 5HLW engine and fitted with 41-seat Strachans bodywork, as a candidate for its future single-deck bus. Although stylish, it was not selected, but it nevertheless gave 12 years' solid service, just surviving the final rebodied Arabs to become A&D's last Guy.

In 1945 three Weymann 'utility'-bodied vehicles were supplied on Guy Arab II chassis. Due to their metal-framed construction they retained their original bodies throughout their lives, although 886 received a new upper deck after an accident in 1955. No 885 (EOR 375) stands behind the Empire Cinema car park in Wellington Avenue, Aldershot, in March 1957, after arriving on service 20C from Ash Street. It was withdrawn from service 16 months later. *Tony Wright*

The final batch of six Guy Arab IIs, delivered towards the end of 1945, were still obviously 'utility' vehicles, although they were a little less angular than previous Strachans-bodied Guys. EOT 30 is about to negotiate the sharp turn from Railway Esplanade, Guildford, into Farnham Road, prior to tackling the long climb to Onslow Village, in May 1948. In 1954 all six were fitted with new 8ft-wide, 56-seat East Lancs bodies, allowing them to serve for another 11 years before withdrawal. *V. C. Jones*

23

Aldershot's Wellington Avenue was the terminus for eight local routes as well as the important service 20 to Guildford. Heading a row of buses is 867 (EHO 173); this was the first Guy Arab delivered to the company, in 1942, and was rebodied with this 51-seat Weymann body in 1950. Behind are an un-rebuilt Guy Arab and one of the 1938 Dennis Lance IIs. *Martin Brown*

24

Six of the 'utility'-bodied Guy Arab II series delivered late in 1945 were rebodied in 1954 by East Lancs with 56-seat bodywork similar to that on the Dennis Lance K4 series (LOU 31-50). However, the chassis were 7ft 6in wide, so the 8ft bodies fitted seemed rather cumbersome. These vehicles were usually to be found on services 1, 2 and 3C (Aldershot–Camberley–Egham). No 888 (EOT 25) is pictured in Aldershot bus station. *Tony Wright collection*

Guy Arab 868 (EHO 217) of 1942, with its body replaced by Weymann in 1950, is seen emerging from a side road near the National Gas Turbine Establishment, Pyestock, while on a tour for the Railway Enthusiast's Club of Farnborough. *Gruffydd Evans*

The lower-deck interior of 868 (EHO 217), which had a new (1950) Weymann body on its 1942 Guy Arab chassis, shows clearly the offside sunken gangway and the Clayton heater on the front bulkhead. The grey woodwork shown was originally given a more pleasing grained-wood effect. *Gruffydd Evans*

The unique Guy Arab LUF, 186 (KOT 113), a 41-seat rear-entrance bus with the only single-deck East Lancs body in the fleet, was bought in 1953 as a possible future standard vehicle. It is pictured in The Grove at Aldershot, opposite the bus station.
In the background is the works of Gale & Polden, printers. At one time they supplied the needs of the Army — as well as civilian organisations in the area — and photographed every significant event in and around the town. *Tony Wright collection*

27

3. Underfloor Engines

In the early 1950s things were changing at A&D. In common with other operators, the company had identified the benefits of the underfloor-engine concept for increasing seating capacity, but the single-deck fleet remained essentially of prewar designs. The evaluation of the Dennis and Guy prototype underfloor-engined candidates, as well as the Atkinson Alpha and Leyland Tiger Cub, had proved unsuccessful, and there was considerable delay in the implementation of A&D's replacement programme. However, after a further service trial A&D selected the AEC Reliance MU3RV chassis for its next generation of coaches and single-deck buses. The MU3RV chassis was 8ft wide and 30ft long, with five-speed synchromesh gearbox and vacuum brakes. However, the A&D specification called for the smaller 6.75-litre AH410 engine, in preference to the 7.75-litre AH470 used by other operators. During the next 15 years we came to appreciate the range of Reliance vehicles and gradually accepted them as the new standard-bearer for A&D coach and single-deck bus requirements.

A&D's AEC Reliance MU3RV coaches (MOR 581-605) entered service in 1954, fitted with 41-seat, centre-entrance Strachans 'Everest' coachwork, which maintained the traditional high level of interior comfort. The modern, box-like styling was completely new to A&D, however, and caused some critics to suggest that the square shape resembled a horsebox rather than a coach! The high, straight chassis frame and the associated high floor enabled views over hedges and garden walls — a new experience when travelling by coach. However, the disadvantage was the unusually high waistline, which reduced the size of the windows and overall visibility. In an effort to improve performance, several of these coaches had the AH410 engine replaced in 1958 by the more powerful AH470 type. In later years they were used for excursions and stage-carriage services, but by

the 1960s, with the spread of one-man operation, the centre-entrance layout was not viable for bus operation, so in 1967 no fewer than 15 (MOR 581/3/5-8/90-3/5, 600/1/3/4) had their coach bodies replaced with Metro-Cammell bus bodywork.

The bus version of the Reliance MU3RV entered A&D service in 1957 (RCG 601-30), these being followed by further examples (SOU 421-43) in 1958. The front-entrance body design was to BET specification and was manufactured by Weymann. This represented a new alliance, as Weymann (and, latterly, its successor Metro-Cammell-Weymann) would body A&D Reliance buses for the next 11 years. However, the specific A&D feature which delighted many was the gold A&D scroll emblazoned on the cream waist panels which extended across the frontal area just below the windscreen and below the forward

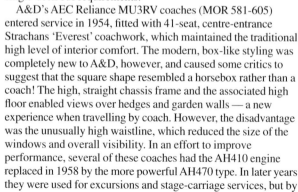

Before and after. In September 1968, opposite A&D's Guildford garage, 251 (MOR 582) retains its original 41-seat Strachans coach body, while neighbour 549 (MOR 590) has received a new 40-seat bus body from Metro-Cammell-Weymann. No 251 was withdrawn from service at the end of the month, but its companion continued in service for some years with Alder Valley. *Peter Trevaskis*

41- and 43-seat AEC Reliances started to replace the long-favoured Dennis single-deck buses from March 1957, when 30 of them entered service within a few weeks. Weymann-bodied 286 (RCG 604) stands alongside similar 297 (RCG 615) in Aldershot bus station when new. The AEC chassis was to become the norm for single-deck buses and coaches until the introduction of the Bristol RELL in 1970, at which time the last of the 1957 Reliances were withdrawn. *Tony Wright*

▲ passenger window on each side of the body. The seating layout was dependent upon type of operation, with 43 seats for crew operation and only 41 for one-man operation. But to passengers the most noticeable difference was in the ride, which represented a significant improvement on that of earlier A&D single-deck buses. The five-speed synchromesh gearbox, meanwhile, was a first for A&D buses; gone were the days of double de-clutching, and all gear changes were swift and smooth. The driver would often have a smile on his face as he confidently changed gear, although he appeared less comfortable as he used all his driving skill to overcome the lack of power, especially on an incline. Forty years later, as owners of a former A&D Reliance, the authors learned that power relates to engine revs, and, although we concentrated on avoiding the engine

labouring, we drove more typically with the accelerator fully depressed to the floor.

The Reliance MU3RV was superseded in 1960 by the 2MU3RV type (1960 batch: XHO 370-7; 1961 batch: 378-93 AOU), which in single-deck bus form was fitted with 41- or 43-seat standard BET bodywork by Weymann. The 2MU3RV buses were fitted with single-plate-glass drivers' windscreens, which marked a significant departure from previous practice; this resulted from changes in legislation in 1960 which rescinded the need for a split (partially opening) windscreen to be fitted on the driver's side, and all future single-deck buses and coaches had single-piece driver's windscreens.

Fifteen Reliance 2MU3RV coaches (414-28 DHO) entered service in 1962, fitted with Park Royal 'dual-purpose' coachwork.

The 41-seat, front-entrance, 30ft-long bodywork closely resembled the Weymann single-deck bus, albeit with improved styling and a new A&D livery, with the body above the (lowered) waistline painted cream; this was very stylish when compared with the earlier Everest coach, which had by then become very dated. However, as the result of changes in the Traffic Regulations in 1962, which permitted the operation of 36ft-long coaches, the 2MU3RV coaches were withdrawn from premium A&D coach services after only a year and modified for one-man operation on stage-carriage service.

To benefit from the new 36ft length regulation, in 1963 A&D introduced 15 Reliance 4MU4RA coaches (466-80 FCG) powered by the AH470 engine. These were fitted with a stretched (49-seat) and more curvaceous version of the earlier Park Royal body, with wrap-around windscreens at both front and rear. As passengers, we felt the increased power and performance, especially in the one coach fitted with the experimental 8.2-litre AH505 engine.

In 1966 five 6MU3RA Reliances arrived (FHO 531-5D), fitted with 49-seat Weymann coachwork to the same design as was used on the previous Park Royal-bodied 4MU4RA models. Powered by the AH505 engine driving through a five-speed synchromesh gearbox, these provided further speed and reduced journey times. The single-deck bus version, again bodied by the MCW group (but at the Metro-Cammell works in Birmingham, following the closure of Weymann's Addlestone factory), entered service in 1967 (HHO 536-42E) — the last time A&D favoured MCW for new single-deck buses. It was a great relief

No 415 (415 DHO) was the second of 15 AEC Reliances delivered in 1962 with 41-seat dual-purpose Park Royal bodies. For a year they were used on the London express service, before being displaced by longer 49-seat coaches. Ten of them were sold on to City of Oxford Motor Services in 1969/70. *Geoffrey Morant*

to many when, in 1967, A&D commenced replacement of the
AH410 engine with the more powerful AH470 type in the fleet
of older Reliance single-deck buses.

In 1968 there was a step-change in comfort levels when the
latest Reliance 6MU3R coaches (NAA 563-5F) arrived, fitted
with the AH505 engine, five-speed synchromesh gearbox and
49-seat Duple (Northern) Commander III coachwork, making
them ideal for long-distance touring. The same year saw the
arrival of the 36ft single-deck bus in the form of five 6MU3R
Reliances (MOR 558-62F) fitted with 51-seat front-entrance
Willowbrook bodywork; the longest single-deckers ever operated
by A&D, these could carry more passengers than earlier double-
deckers. Bodywork was to the new BET Group dual-purpose
design, which provided coach-style seating and a high level of
comfort, making such vehicles suitable for long-distance coach
operation as well as local routes. In 1969 A&D introduced its
last batch of 6MU3R single-deck buses (PHO 566-95G), this
time fitted with Marshall 45-seat bodywork, the length having
reverted to 33ft.

By 1970 the level of comfort offered by A&D to coach
passengers was at least comparable to that offered by private

coach operators, and this was demonstrated with the arrival of
five Reliance 6U3ZR models fitted with Duple Commander IV
bodywork (VCG 596-600H), which were similar to the existing
Reliance/Commanders except that they were fitted with the
11.3-litre AH691 engine and ZF six-speed synchromesh gearbox.
The high standard of passenger comfort was maintained by
additional 6U3ZR coaches fitted with 49-seat Plaxton Panorama
Elite coachwork (YCG 101/2J) which entered service in 1971
and were the last Reliances to join the A&D fleet.

A significant change occurred for bus operators in 1969 with
the formation of the National Bus Company, which for the first
time allowed A&D access to Bristol bus chassis. A&D
subsequently developed its single-deck bus fleet around Bristol's
RELL6G and RESL6G chassis, fitted with the Gardner 6HLW
engine and a semi-automatic gearbox. The RELL6G was 36ft
long and first appeared in A&D service during 1970/1 (1970
batch: UOU 601-15H; 1971 batch: YHO 616-30J), fitted with
Marshall 'standee' (44 seated, 20 standing) dual-door bodywork,
again to the BET Group standard. The dual-door concept, with
front entrance and centre exit, was a novelty, but during peak
travelling times we soon appreciated the benefit in improved
passenger embarkation and disembarkation times. For many
A&D travellers it was a new experience to enjoy the very
smooth gear changes afforded by the semi-automatic gearbox,
because no form of automatic gearbox had been used on any
A&D buses since the ill-fated Dennis Dominant.

An additional benefit which A&D gained from membership of
the National Bus Company was access to the products of Eastern
Coach Works, a company which previously was able to supply
bodywork only to nationalised companies. The first ECW-
bodied single-deck buses entered service with A&D in 1971
(YHO 631-6J, CCG 291-6K), being of the shorter (33ft)
RESL6G type with dual-door 'standee' bodywork with only 40
seats but space for 20 standing. We had often admired the RE in
service with other operators, and in A&D livery it looked very
smart, although we were disappointed that it did not carry the
traditional scroll logo, which had been replaced with the later
plain gold-block-lettered *ALDERSHOT & DISTRICT* fleetname. Later
that year there arrived further RESL6G buses (CHO 691-9K),
fitted with dual-door Marshall standee bodywork of the same
passenger capacity as the earlier Eastern Coach Works version.
The entire A&D Bristol single-deck fleet continued in service
following transfer to Alder Valley, along with 35 AEC Reliance
coaches and nearly 100 surviving Reliance buses.

The 1969 batch of Reliances were 33ft long and had 45-seat Marshall bodywork, as shown by 569 (PHO 569G) on route 52 from Camberley to Basingstoke — the western extremity of A&D territory — where connections could be made with services operated by Wilts & Dorset and Thames Valley. *Tony Wright collection*

The arrival in the second half of 1971 of the first batch of Bristol buses, with Eastern Coach Works bodywork, enabled services such as the 48A to be operated by one person. No 646 (CCG 291K), a 40-seat RESL6G, is depicted in Chertsey during A&D's final month, December 1971. *Philip Wallis*

Adorned with the straight fleetname introduced in 1967, 560 (MOR 560F), one of the five dual-purpose AEC Reliances delivered in May 1968 with 51-seat Willowbrook bodywork, leaves Aldershot bus station on local service 76 to Cove (Fox Lane Estate). These were the highest-capacity single-deckers ever operated by A&D.
Geoffrey Morant

One of the 1970 consignment of AEC Reliance coaches, 597 (VCG 597H) carried 49 passengers in its Duple Commander IV body, initially on the Farnham–London express service.
The 'Londons' didn't use the bus station at Aldershot but stopped instead in The Grove, where the vehicle is seen in June 1972. *Les Smith*

A new departure for Aldershot & District was the delivery in 1970 of a batch of 15 36ft Bristol RELL6G buses with Marshall dual-door 'standee' bodywork seating 44 and with space for 20 standing passengers. A further 36 Bristols, of both RELL6G and the shorter RESL6G type, were taken into stock before A&D's demise. No 613 (UOU 613H) is pictured on service 31 (Farnham–Guildford via the Hog's Back). *Roy Marshall / Photobus*

4. 'Tracco' in Town

As the name of the company suggests, the heart and main hub of the A&D operation was in the north-Hampshire town of Aldershot, with additional major hubs at Guildford and Woking. Since we authors lived in Cove and Godalming, our experiences were mainly of Aldershot and Guildford respectively. Like many youngsters who were allowed their first taste of freedom, we remember with great excitement our trips on our own into town, five miles away on the bus. Very often we would travel on a Saturday to look around the town for new books or Dinky toys to add to our collection. Occasionally we would take photographs, with our newly acquired Kodak Brownie 127, of some of the buses in the bus station or through the gap in the fence at the back of the depot yard in Halimote Road. The journey from Cove seemed quite a long one, though it was actually only 26 minutes from start to finish. From home we would catch the single-decker

on route 3D, which took us through Cove village, Farnborough, North Camp and along the Queen's Avenue into town.

From Aldershot the bus routes radiated out along 'corridors' of main roads to reach other towns such as Reading, Egham, Midhurst, Woking, Farnham, Alton, Camberley, Guildford, Fleet, Petersfield, Winchester and Basingstoke. Around the western outskirts of Farnborough the rapid postwar development of housing reflected the importance of the area. Contemporary timetables illustrate this growth in the Fifties, when route 76, for example, was a Saturdays-only service from North Camp to West Heath Estate but was soon to become an hourly weekday service, extended from Aldershot to Fox Lane Estate. The 'corridors' to Cove and Camberley became very busy on Saturdays, with a double-decker every eight minutes between Aldershot and Camberley and a bus every 10 minutes between

Comparison. Thames Valley Bristol Lodekka 845 (WJB 229) and A&D Dennis Loline III/Weymann 485 (485 KOT) at Reading Stations when new in 1964. The Loline was built under licence from Bristol using a number of Dennis parts.
Philip Wallis

Alexander-bodied Dennis Loline III 408 (408 COR) emerges from Winchester bus station on a service 14 'short' to Alresford. Most of the 'shorts' between Winchester and Alresford came into being when Winchester & District's licence was taken over in April 1953. *A. J. Douglas*

Having detoured on its service 1 journey from Egham to Aldershot to call at Camberley station, Dennis Lance K4 232 (LOU 60), with Weymann bodywork, stops in London Road, Camberley, to pick up on 1 August 1964. *Tim Stubbs*

No 292 (RCG 610), a 1957 AEC Reliance, in The Borough, Farnham, waits to turn right into Castle Street at the end of its regular journey on service 45 from Elstead. Such a manœuvre would be impossible today, as a result of Farnham's one-way system. *John Aldridge*

A 1961 AEC Reliance with 43-seat Weymann body, 381 (381 AOU) seen in South Street, Farnham (which until 1967 took traffic in both directions), on service 17 from Grayshott to Ewshott. The Farnham–Ewshott part of this route was once a separate service (38). *John Aldridge*

36ft-long Willowbrook-bodied AEC Reliance 559 (MOR 559F) passes Aldershot Police Station in the High Street, working a 3D service to Cove, Minley Estate. Five of these smart-looking dual-purpose vehicles were acquired by A&D in 1968 for use on routes needing their higher seating capacity. *Photobus*

Brand-new Dennis Loline 343 (SOU 451) enters West Street, Farnham, on service 14 to Winchester — the first route to receive these vehicles, from 1 March 1958. Upon repaint they lost their black lining-out, while another modification — possibly at the request of lower-deck passengers — was the removal of the indicators to a position adjacent to the cream strip beneath the windows.
D. Clark / Eric Surfleet collection

Double-deckers did not start operating into Castle Street, Farnham, until 1950 — services 10A (Farnham–Rowledge), 40 (Farnham–Ash Green–Aldershot) and 43 (Farnham–Badshot Lea–Aldershot). The 'natives' were up in arms at the prospect, assuming that upper-deck passengers would be able to peer into their bedrooms! Rebuilt Dennis Lance II 741 (CCG 338) carries a 48-seat body by East Lancs in this 1951 view.
David Sharwood

Aldershot and Cove during the heydays of the late Fifties and early Sixties.

The importance of Aldershot in those days as a typical focal point for local shopping showed clearly the contemporary way of life. Our grandparents often made a special outing to Aldershot on the 44 from Frimley Green. First stop in town was for a coffee in Thomas White's, the department store! This was the highlight of their week. After working through the week, this was the only spare day for family shopping, before the advent of Sunday shopping and local out-of-town supermarkets. We remember being caught out by missing the bus home from Aldershot as it sailed by already full at the Queen Hotel stop, at the end of town. A late return home and a cold dinner soon taught us to walk round from the shops to the bus station and join the long queue in the hope of catching the bus. If all else failed and we were lucky, a duplicate bus would be provided. This too would soon be full and sail by all stops until it reached Farnborough. A very

crowded Aldershot bus station was quite common on Saturdays, although weekdays had their busy moments as well. It was fun to see the Inspector arrange the duplicates, and for a few minutes we were puzzled, wondering what unusual bus we might have for the homeward journey. Hopefully, in place of a Lancet with rear sliding door, it would be one of the rare front- or centre-entrance single-deckers on which we could sit near the driver and pretend to take the controls!

One joy for the young Cove traveller was the thrill of travelling upstairs on route 3A. The downside to this excitement was the 'long' walk from Cove village to home; double-deckers could not go beyond that point because of the low West Heath railway bridge. Ironically, an improved bridge came too late — in 1962, when passenger numbers were lower and double-deckers were not really needed on the route.

The bus station still did not provide the focus for all travellers, as some routes going in the Farnham direction started in the

In June 1964 Camberley High Street still had two-way traffic but was already congested (witness the vans parked on the pavement). No 227 (LOU 55) was a 1954 Dennis Lance K4 with 56-seat lowbridge Weymann Orion body. Service 2, between Aldershot and Camberley, was one of three which combined to provide a 15min frequency between the two towns.
Tim Stubbs

Miles away from Ewshott Camp, and not on a service 39 either, 231 (LOU 59), a Weymann-bodied Dennis Lance K4, was photographed in Petersfield Square not long before withdrawal in January 1965. Based at Woking depot, it had been hired for an enthusiasts' tour, but had no appropriate route blinds.
Les Smith

Seen in Winchester Broadway, having just set out from the bus station, 341 (SOU 449) heads for Aldershot on service 14. This 33-mile route was the first to be allocated these new Dennis Lolines, from 1 March 1958. *Geoffrey Morant*

Pictured by the Swan Hotel in Alton High Street, 242 (LOU 70) was a Dennis Falcon P5 of 1954. The picture was taken in 1965, shortly before it was sold out of service. These 30-seaters continued the tradition of small buses operating from Alton depot, which started in the 1920s. *John Aldridge*

On 30 July 1966 (the day England won the World Cup) Dennis Falcon P5 247 (LOU 75) almost obscures the Southdown enquiry and booking office in Petersfield, where A&D outstationed a bus for its service 6 (Aldershot–Petersfield–Steep) in the Southdown depot. The latter company ran several services from the town, most notably to Portsmouth and Southsea, while Hants & Dorset also had two services into the town including the 67 from Winchester, on which one of its Bristol MWs is seen alongside. The 53 has its destination blind already set for its return journey across country to Alton. *Philip Wallis*

High Street (routes 10, 32 and 43), while those heading in the Guildford direction started in Wellington Avenue (20, 35, 35A, 42 and 42A). The London, excursion and coastal journeys called at The Grove, adjacent to the bus station. In March 1950 the bus station was extended: the original section was retained, and two new through platforms were built on an area enlarged beyond the southwestern boundary. This allowed the inclusion of the long-distance bus route 19 to Midhurst, Chichester and Bognor Regis as part of the terminus, after many years when it began its long journey from the Queen Hotel. As well as serving other towns, Aldershot buses connected the intermediate villages and communities such as Crookham, Crondall, Hindhead, Ash, Frimley, Brookwood, and Odiham. There were local town services which reached North Town (routes 20B and 20D) and the Bathing Pool (42 and 42A). The latter was always shown on the blinds as 'Circular Route'. We knew what that meant, but we wonder if it meant much to any strangers in town.

For much of the early Fifties the 'Tracco' was expanding, reflecting demand as well as the takeover of smaller companies. Unfortunately an emergency timetable had to be introduced in 1956 due to the fuel shortages and rationing which resulted from the Suez Crisis, and fewer journeys could be made into town on Sundays and during the evenings. This, combined with a strike in 1957 and the increased ownership of private cars, put a stop to the growth in passenger numbers; like many others, our family bought their first car, and we relied less on the buses for trips to town.

We have memories of journeys to school either on service or on special bus services, which were exciting as well. Often one of the Everest-bodied AEC coaches replaced a normal service bus, spending time away from coach travel to help out on stage duties. The Fifties and Sixties saw a regular convoy of six double-deckers taking boys from Aldershot to Farnborough Grammar School and girls from Farnborough to Aldershot High School. Various Lances — K3s and K4s — and Lolines were sent on these school runs. The towns were inextricably linked for many years by this daily transport arrangement.

The other main towns served by the company were 'at the other end of the planet' for us. A trip to Guildford or Woking was rare and exciting. The excitement came when we saw other buses in the fleet, since buses were rarely transferred between depots. Another attraction to us was the sight of buses belonging to other operators — London Transport served parts of those towns, while Thames Valley served Reading and Camberley.

Guildford grew up as a Surrey market town on the River Wey. A&D had two inter-linked main terminals in the town in our time — Onslow Street and Farnham Road, the latter a replacement for on-street parking in Park Street. Opened on 23 June 1949, Onslow Street bus station was built adjacent to the original Dennis works. Several photographs record the layout, which consisted of three four-berth platforms and a layover area. Nearly one year later, on 11 May 1950, the second station alongside Farnham Road was opened. This had three long platforms with continuous shelters, serving 14 bus stands, as well as a booking office and a staff room.

Most routes from Guildford went along 'corridors' to such places as Cranleigh, Horsham, Ewhurst, Farncombe, Godalming and Petersfield, as well as to Aldershot and Woking. Again, there were town services, operated in competition with small local companies — for example Safeguard, which ran to the Cathedral and Westborough. London Transport served the northern and eastern directions from town — an arrangement settled by an Act of Parliament in 1933. Like Farnborough, Guildford had its fair share of growth in small estates in the postwar period, and all required a regular and reliable bus service for shopping, work and social activities.

Another Surrey town, Woking, which was the smallest A&D hub, did not have a bus station, the terminus for A&D and LT routes being on the road adjacent to the north side of the railway station. Here A&D's 'Brabs', K3s and Guy Arabs waited to take people to such places as Horsell, Chobham, Sunningdale, West End and Blackdown Camp. Frustratingly, the buses were partially hidden from the rail passenger's view by the station's perimeter wall!

No 171 (HOT 700) was one of the final batch of Dennis Lance K3 51-seaters, delivered late in 1950. It is shown travelling towards its Farnham Road bus station terminus in Guildford, ready to return to Chertsey on service 48 on 22 September 1962. Nothing remains of this street scene today.
Peter Trevaskis

HOU 911 — a 1950 Dennis Lancet J10 — was one of the first A&D buses to carry a fleet number (185) from new. Towards the end of its life it was based at Woking depot and is depicted at Guildford's Farnham Road bus station in December 1966.
Brian Oxborough

In August 1969 rebodied AEC Reliance 546 (MOR 586) stands at the terminus of service 55A, alongside Woking station, on layover. The local A&D inspectors referred to this line of stops (which included those for London Transport) as 'the rank'. *Brian Oxborough*

Guildford's Onslow Street bus station in 1972. Although in green A&D livery, 1971 ECW-bodied Bristol RESL 650 (CCG 295K) has now passed to Alder Valley, as its red fleet-number plate (457) reveals. The Friary Brewery, in the background, pinpoints the site of today's Friary Shopping Centre. The vehicle on the left is another RESL, but with a Marshall body, 631 (CHO 691K).. *Photobus*

A scene at The Broadway, by Woking station. On the left is 546 (MOR 586), previously a 41-seat, centre-entrance Strachans-bodied coach but now sporting a new 40-seat bus body built in 1967 by Metro-Cammell. To the right is an earlier Reliance bus, 335 (SOU 443), dating from 1958, with 41-seat bodywork by Weymann. *John Aldridge collection*

Guildford's Farnham Road bus station *c*1970, with Marshall-bodied AEC Reliance 566 (PHO 566G) departing for Horsham on service 33 and Dennis Loline III 430 (122 DOR) destined for Aarons Hill Estate, Godalming. Every building in this picture has since vanished!

5. 'Tracco' in the Countryside

One of our clearest recollections is of browsing through each new timetable and looking at the folded map of routes to find any changes. The 'Tracco' reached a vast network of villages and small rural communities. Places such as Newton Valence, Medstead, Beech and East Tisted, served by infrequent bus services from the mid-Hampshire market town of Alton, conjured up pictures of remote farmland and isolated hamlets, miles away and rarely seen. Apart from the towns mentioned in the previous chapter, vast tracts of farmland, countryside and wild areas were included in Aldershot & District territory. Without the buses, many villages and hamlets might not have survived so well, so dependent were they on public transport for carrying people, shopping and parcels.

Around the three main centres of Aldershot, Guildford and Woking were acres of open countryside, often protected from any further development because of their use for military training. This meant that on any journeys into town one would pass through typical scenes of Scots pine, silver birch and general scrubland, suitable for night manœuvres and Army exercises. In one way it enabled residents to see the countryside on their doorsteps. On the other hand it must have been a considerable barrier to housing development and potential growth for our favourite bus company.

Most routes which penetrated into the countryside started from one of the three main centres. As passenger numbers were often low, single-deckers were almost always used on these routes. From Guildford there were services to the far reaches of the network, at Wisborough Green, Ewhurst and Horsham, each passing through acres of countryside. Routes 33 and 33A from Guildford served small communities like Baynards, Rudgwick and Bucks Green. The long journey to Horsham involved reversing up a lane at Bucks Green and doubling-back through the village on its way. All these local communities, as elsewhere, depended upon the company's buses to bring parcels and take people to the nearest town for vital shopping and leisure requirements. A similar corridor of countryside was fed by the long route 14

In March 1960 AEC Reliance 305 (RCG 623) stands at the Hare & Hounds, Rowledge — terminus of service 10A from Farnham (Castle Street). This was probably the Sunday when the route was converted to one-man operation. Note the large A&D timetable frame displayed on the wall of the pub. *Peter Trevaskis*

from Aldershot to Winchester. On that route there was plenty of forest and farmland around places like Bentley, Alresford and Kingsworthy. Unusually, the 'main road' route 14 was normally operated by double-deckers, presumably because of the busier sections between Aldershot and Farnham, around Alton and between Winchester and Alresford. However, it often travelled for miles through open country without picking up anyone.

As well as routes emanating from the urban centres there were some interesting infrequent cross-country routes in the timetable, notably the curious network of services around one of the southern extremities of the network, at Petworth. Service 51 went from Haslemere through Fisher Street — a tiny hamlet clinging to a crossroads on a main road — and Northchapel (another very small village) to the market town of Petworth. The neighbouring but isolated hamlets of Balls Cross, Kirdford, Plaistow and Loxwood were served by infrequent routes 50, 50A and 60. When people used rural services they found that the bus was often staffed by the same crew, who as a result were well known to the passengers. This relationship is demonstrated by

the experience of one former employee, who retells the story of the times when the buses through Kirdford and Shillinglee were often full of shopping baskets with lists — but no people. Apparently, the locals would stand and wait for the bus and put their shopping order on board; the obliging driver would then take these into Petworth and on the return journey would drop off the loaded baskets, filled by the shopkeeper in town. These regular transactions went on for years, through the Fifties and into the early Sixties. The same driver recalls the times when route 60 would 'divert' into the apple-packing station at Kirdford to collect regular orders for passengers and crew. Such reminiscences of this particular area illustrate what was typical countryside activity at the time.

Close examination of the folded timetable maps showed other intricate cross-country networks of routes, such as route 17 between Ewshot and Tilford, which brought passengers from the outlying villages to the market town of Farnham. Typically, this rural service had an impact on the social life of those living in the country areas. If one missed the bus when in town, there

Plaistow church forms the backdrop for Dennis Falcon P5 275 (POR 421) *en route* from Godalming to Petworth. During his layover at Petworth the driver will carry out 'shopping duty' for some of the residents along this route! Most unusually for a single-decker, 275 was later converted into a tree-cutter. *Mike Stephens*

Dennis Falcon P5 248 (LOU 76) awaits departure from Medstead church for its journey back to Alton on service 54. At one time the 54 continued beyond Medstead to serve Bentworth, but that section of the route was withdrawn in 1952. *Mike Stephens*

Aldershot depot regularly provided the duplicate bus for the later stages of the 8.00am Guildford–Aldershot journey on service 20; the vehicle would travel empty out to Normandy, where it would await the service bus. On 11 November 1958 this duty was performed by Dennis Lance K3 133 (GOU 833), seen just off of the main A323 in Hunts Hill Road. *Peter Trevaskis*

Diverting from the main A33 Reading–Basingstoke road, Dennis Lance K4 220 (LOU 48) calls at Swallowfield village on 29 September 1964. Service 12, on which this particular vehicle was frequently to be seen, did not serve the village until 1 May 1954, when it became a joint operation with the Thames Valley Traction Co. No 220 is now in preservation and has been seen many times in its old familiar haunts. *Peter Trevaskis*

For many years the Plume of Feathers pub at Crondall (to the nearside of Dennis Loline III 483, *en route* from Basingstoke to Aldershot) had traces of green paint upon its jutting wall where less-experienced drivers misjudged the turn. This view dates from May 1969.
Peter Trevaskis

A short distance along the main A3 London Road from the company's Hindhead garage was its booking office and waiting room, opposite the Royal Huts Hotel. Here the important north–south and east–west routes crossed at Huts Corner. Here Dennis Loline 368 (SOU 476) calls *en route* from Grayswood to Whitehill on service 18 on Sunday 11 June 1967. The driver is probably visiting the office while awaiting the arrival of a connecting service.
Philip Wallis

would be a long wait for the next one. Of greater importance was the relatively early departure of the last bus home. To ensure that one could catch it after going to the pictures, for example, one needed to be seated in the cinema during the first performance before the end of the main film so as to leave at the same point in the second showing for the homeward journey. From Farnham another set of routes, originally operated by Yellow Bus Services, went to Guildford through the villages nestling in the shadow of the Hog's Back. Routes 65 and 66 went through Seale, Puttenham and Compton — all little changed to this day.

It is surprising to discover that the infamous 'bus wars' of pre-regulation days affected the countryside as well as the town services, as it is hard to imagine a large company wanting to establish services on thinly populated routes in competition with rival small firms. However, from the market town of Alton (to take a good example) A&D set up three routes — to

Petersfield, to Medstead and Bentworth and to East Tisted — in competition with 'Ruby Queen' of Chawton, a village on the outskirts of Alton. Presumably the extensive network of busy town services compensated for such poorly loaded routes. Indeed, in the days before market research, routes were determined by traditional market days rather than public demand. For many years there was a route from Alton to the tiny community of Newton Valence; originally this was quite frequent, with a couple of journeys each way on weekdays, but, as car ownership increased, the service was reduced to one journey each way once a week, followed by the inevitable demise of transport to this destination, only four miles from Alton. This illustration serves to tell the overall story of rural transport during the period of the 'glory days'.

As described in Chapter 1, the company operated a series of small vehicles such as Dennis Aces and Falcons, and, while a few

Service 64 between Woking and Fox Corner was suspended on the outbreak of World War 2 and did not resume until March 1948. Seen on 11 September 1958, Dennis Falcon P3 151 (GOU 851) has just departed from its Fox Corner terminus and is about to cross the A322 at Worplesdon War Memorial — a manœuvre that is now impossible. The service was never very profitable and was finally abandoned just 10 days later, on 21 September 1958. *David Sharwood*

When service 13 commenced in 1924 it ran between Haslemere and Alton and ran straight on along the road in the background (now the B3004) to Lindford before reaching Bordon. It was later diverted onto the road shown in this early-1960s photograph taken at Standford Lodge. The blinds on Dennis Falcon 281 (POR 427) are incorrectly set; service 13 ran via Kingsley, while the 13A ran via Oakhanger. *Hans Retallick*

of these valuable workhorses were to be seen on urban routes (notably Farnborough local route 61, which served the town's narrower side streets), they were more readily associated with rural services, being ideally suited to narrow country lanes. In later years 32-seater Lancet J3s were to be seen on country routes, especially cross-country services like the 45 from Farnham to Godalming. This was a route where the motion of the bus weaving along the twisting roads caused some people to suffer regularly from travel sickness. Country folk had also to cope with the single-deckers' sliding doors. We have vivid memories of attempting to grab the vertical handle to pull it back to open the rear door if the conductor happened to be near the front of the bus. Alternatively, the doors would sometimes slide open when the bus was travelling along and

while the conductor was at the front, leaving passengers struggling to shut the heavy door. Always the door seemed to be stiff, and our fear was that the driver would move off before we could open it to alight at our intended destination. Of course, the new wave of AEC Reliances, with their electrically operated doors, helped considerably; sometimes they were used on quieter country routes, especially around Tilford, Farncombe and the villages southeast of Guildford, bringing the delights of modern buses to these rural communities. However, it is surprising that they could be manœuvred around the narrow lanes encountered on the remoter parts of their journeys, and we admired the skill of the drivers who negotiated such lanes without scraping the banks and walls, especially when confronted with oncoming traffic.

One of the second batch of Dennis Falcon P5s, 280 (POR 426) passes over Somerset Bridge, which spans the River Wey, between Shackleford and Elstead, in late 1970. Service 46 ran from Farncombe to Elstead. *Brian Oxborough*

Dennis Falcon P5 281 (POR 427) has reached the halfway point on its 46 journey from Cock Hill, Elstead, to Godalming. The view was posed for the photographer at Shackleford (Shop). *Mike Stephens*

6. Highdays and Holidays

Prior to the mid-1950s few people owned or routinely travelled by car, and the coach was the main means of travelling any distance by road, and those of us in the A&D operating area relied solely on the faithful A&D coach services to celebrate highdays and holidays. In those days travelling by coach was a real treat, and with no motorway network until the 1960s all coach journeys were time-consuming. With increased car ownership and the introduction of the motorways, travelling long distances became much easier. However, in spite of improved coach design over the years, the car gradually replaced the coach for day trips and holiday travel.

Introduced in 1928, A&D's London express service — or 'the London', as we affectionately knew it — was the company's premier coach service, using its latest and most luxurious vehicles. During our 'glory days' the Farnham service operated to a frequent, all-year-round timetable from Farnham to Victoria Coach Station, picking up at points along the A30 as far as Egham before running limited-stop to London. The arrival of new coaches in the fleet caused us great excitement and was tempered only by the loss of the by-then familiar existing coaches, which were relegated to less-prestigious service, often ending their days as humble buses on stage-carriage services. The exhilaration of a 'London' pulling into Victoria Coach Station's Bay 1 — A&D's allocated space — can still be recalled; this was the primary bay, close to the entrance, refreshments and toilets and not too far to run when late for the return journey. Our arrival brought us to the hub of the UK coach network, with connections for all major towns, cities and seaside resorts. Unfortunately at peak times the 'Londons' were in high demand, especially return journeys, and occasionally we had to travel on a stage-carriage bus — sometimes a double-decker — operated as a 'dupe'. Interestingly A&D always used this term (as in 'duplicate') for an additional vehicle for an oversubscribed service and never used the term 'relief' officially. During the summer,

A&D coaches and stage-carriage buses often operated in support of the Royal Blue express service from Victoria to the main holiday resorts in the West Country.

For many local people, experience of travel on A&D coaches came in the form of the coastal service, excursions or private hire — the main elements of A&D's coaching business. The coastal service, introduced in 1928, operated from June to September, with daily services from Camberley, via Aldershot, to Portsmouth and Southsea, Bognor and Littlehampton, Brighton and Worthing and Eastbourne, and from Woking, via Guildford, to Portsmouth and Southsea, Bognor, Brighton and Eastbourne. The service was very useful because it not only facilitated day trips but also provided a connection with the

Parked in a side street near Victoria Coach Station during the late 1930s is COR 156, one of the 1938 Dennis Lancet II coaches used on the express service from Farnham. These vehicles were among the first in A&D's fleet to have oil engines and were fitted with luxurious 32-seat bodywork by Strachans. After demotion to stage services during the war, they were reconditioned to re-start the London service in June 1946.
W. J. Haynes / Southdown Enthusiasts' Club

Not long after entering service in 1948, gleaming Dennis Lancet J3 coach GAA 615 receives attention in Castle Street, Farnham, prior to setting out for Victoria Coach Station. *Douglas Hawkins*

An interior view of one of the 15 Dennis Lancet J3 coaches delivered in 1948 for use on the Farnham–London express service. Fitted with 32-seat Strachans bodywork, these vehicles also saw service on excursions and 'coastals' before being withdrawn *en bloc* at the end of September 1961. Note the prominent Clayton heater on the front bulkhead and the stylish lights on each window pillar. *Peter Trevaskis*

Dennis Lancet J10c coach 200 (LAA 235), in its first month of service in June 1953, stands in Castle Street, Farnham, prior to departure on the London express service. Full front excepted, its 38-seat Strachans body shows a close affinity with previous coaches from the same builder. It did not long remain in this livery of dark green upper half and light green lower, as the colours were subsequently reversed. These vehicles spent little more than a year in front-line service before being replaced by the AEC Reliances. *David Sharwood*

For many years the company's Farnham–London express service was allocated stand No 1 at Victoria Coach Station. This view, from March 1956, shows AEC Reliance coach 250 (MOR 581), then just 18 months old. This vehicle is now preserved, albeit in a substantially different form, having been rebodied by Metro-Cammell in 1967 as a 40-seater bus. *Peter Trevaskis*

Passing through Staines on the express coach service from Victoria Coach Station to Farnham, 251 (MOR 582) was one of the 25 Strachans-bodied AEC Reliances delivered in 1954. This particular vehicle was one of the 10 which were not subsequently rebodied and was withdrawn soon after this photograph was taken in 1968. *John Aldridge*

Passing Steyne Gardens in Worthing, 193 (LAA 228) is part of a 'coastal' convoy returning from Brighton during the busy summer holiday period. The drivers of these 38-seat Dennis Lancet coaches referred to them as 'sweat boxes', due to the enclosed nature of their cabs. *Tony Wright collection*

South Coast Express service operated by Southdown, allowing access to other resorts on the South Coast. Those passengers who lived along the corridor served by A&D stage-carriage service 19, which operated from Aldershot via Farnham, Hindhead, Haslemere, Midhurst and Chichester to Bognor, probably used this service for their seaside outings — especially the limited-stop 19A variant, which operated during the summer months from 1958 to 1969. The range of summer full-day excursions extended from other seaside resorts, such as Bournemouth, to The Derby, Goodwood and other race meetings and visits to towns and cities of historical interest, such as Salisbury and Stratford-upon-Avon, especially after the takeover of Comfy Coaches of Farnham. In addition there were half-day trips to Windsor and Worthing. As the motorway network grew and coach design improved, we enjoyed the more ambitious

long-distance tours operated to Wales. A mystery evening drive operated from Aldershot and Guildford during the summer was always pleasurable, as it was effectively a coach trip to a not-too-distant pub. Afternoon tours were more sedate, in the form of a Hog's Back circular or a visit to London Airport, with a stop for afternoon tea or refreshments. Sunday was the busiest day for excursions, and, apart from those operated in the high season or to race meetings, excursions were seldom run on Monday or Fridays, because of limited demand.

Tickets for the London express service, as well as for all scheduled coach services and excursions, were obtained through advance booking at A&D offices or booking agents in local shops in the area. Pre-booked reservations, tickets, seat allocations and pick-up points were allocated by the chart rooms at A&D offices and the information given to the driver in individual envelopes. This procedure often resulted in pandemonium when the coach arrived at the pick-up point, as we tried first to find our driver and obtain our ticket and then to identify which coach and seat we had been allocated. For private hire the procedure was different: there was no seat allocation, so

With other traffic conspicuous by its absence, Aldershot-bound AEC Reliance 479 (479 FCG) rounds Hyde Park Corner in 1964. Fifteen of these 36ft-long coaches, with 49-seat Park Royal bodies, had been introduced the previous year for use on express services. All survived to be absorbed by Alder Valley in 1972. *Michael Dryhurst*

The annual seaside outing for employees' families and children became a traditional event in the 1930s. After a break during the war years the trips were restarted, but by the 1960s the advent of the family car no doubt had some bearing on the fact that only two coaches were required instead of up to 15 prewar. On 9 August 1966 one of the 1954 Strachans-bodied Reliance coaches and a later (1963) Park Royal-bodied example were used to take 96 adults and children to Bognor Regis. *Peter Holmes collection*

On an evening drive from Guildford on Sunday 13 July 1969, Park Royal-bodied AEC Reliance coach 416 (416 DHO) stands outside the Four Elms at Smithwood Common. As with most Mystery Tours, there was a break for refreshments at a hostelry. Most of the passengers appear reluctant to board for the return journey! *Peter Trevaskis*

the arrival of the coach was followed by a mad dash to clamber aboard in the hope of obtaining the best seats. Private hires (or 'privates') were very popular and offered a broad range of bespoke services available throughout the year as Sunday School, Working Men's Club or pub outings, from day trips to the seaside in summer to visits to London shows and pantomimes etc during the winter. A particular treat for A&D staff was the annual company-subsidised outing to the seaside, with several coachloads of staff and their families setting off from each depot and converging on a seaside resort.

Until the late 1960s, with no motorways and few dual carriageways, coach travel was very simple and slow, with average speeds of 20-30mph and long journey times. There being no in-coach entertainment, no motorway service areas, few cafés and toilets, we boys used our initiative to make the outing a success. On the outward journey we stopped at a café, although on a Sunday School outing — a major event in the 1940s — the coach stopped only to allow us to visit the toilet. With no café stop, many of us had eaten our pre-packed lunches, carefully prepared by our mothers, before the coach had travelled far. On seaside outings there was always great excitement as the cry went up 'I see the sea!', confirming the first person to catch sight of it. Things were very different when we were on a pub or Working Men's Club outing. These tended not to stop at cafés, preferring to carry their own refreshment, usually in the form of crates of beer in the boot. On outward journeys we would stop with the coach parked on the grass verge, by the side of the road, or in a layby, with the men sitting on the crates drinking beer. We youngsters, together with the womenfolk, were left to consume lemonade.

It was common practice on the outward journey of club and pub outings to use the rear nearside tyre and a chalk mark on the bodywork of the coach as the means of selecting the

winning number for the raffle. The tyre was marked in an equal number of sectors to the number of passengers, with each sector allocated a number. When the coach stopped we all hoped we would be the lucky passenger who had the same number as that on the sector coincident with the chalk mark on the bodywork.

On the return journey, irrespective of the type of coach outing, we usually joined in community singing — a popular pastime in those days — with the singing sometimes led by the driver. It was normal practice to stop at a pub, especially on club or pub outings, when the crates by then contained only empty bottles. The men soon disappeared into the pub, with all of us children and some of the mothers left outside anxiously awaiting the arrival of lemonade and crisps (the type which contained the salt in a blue wrapper). Some pubs provided a children's room, but the noise of younger children running around screaming could be deafening, so we preferred to continue the practice of sitting outside. An amusing recollection from those early-postwar days, when there were no service areas *en route*, is the sight of coaches parked by the side of the road or in a layby, with the boys and men hurriedly disappearing from view in one direction and the girls and women heading off in the other; after 10 minutes or so comfort would be restored and all would re-board to resume the journey. Tipping the driver had become a custom, whereby during the final stage of the journey one passenger moved amongst the

A rare rear view of an AEC Reliance coach, 268 (MOR 599), on a private-hire duty in 1957. It shows how, long before legislation appeared, A&D was already experienced in coping with physically disabled passengers, though the high floor level of these vehicles would have been a disadvantage.
Les Smith collection

An outing for Sheerwater Labour Party. Dennis Lancet J10C coach 198 (LAA 233) leads older Dennis Lancet J3 985 (GAA 621) on the long climb up Bury Hill, near Arundel, prior to a refreshment break at the summit — and a cooling-off period for the vehicles!
Ted Gamblin

rest of us with a hat collecting money; in return, we hoped that the tip would influence his stopping the coach close to where we lived, making the final part of our return home easier.

The key element to the success of any coach service — which still applies today — was the driver, who needed to be friendly, attentive and committed to the needs of the passengers. The best of these drivers were always smartly dressed in the A&D uniform to suit the season. Exuding personality, commitment and dedication and paying attention to our every need, they often spent considerable time prior to the journey researching the destination, so that they could offer sound advice and suggestions as to the best places to visit and the best restaurants at which to eat, and were always ready to load suitcases into the boot. The most popular drivers were widely known, and private hirers would frequently specify a particular driver for their outing.

With improvements in the road network and service areas, not to mention vehicle design, A&D's coach services expanded to include longer, more ambitious tours, but somehow the community spirit — the most treasured experience, which we all took for granted in those earlier days — was lost, probably never to return.

7. For King, Queen and Country

Aldershot has always been proud of its position as the 'Home of the British Army', and there were always close links between A&D and the military in providing bus and coach services to troops, both within the town and the surrounding area. This was a special relationship which endured throughout the company's existence.

Thousands of troops from different regiments have been located in the Aldershot Garrison, as well as in the large number of barracks and camps within the Aldershot and Southern Command areas, and the military relied on A&D for their civilian transportation. The military presence in the A&D operating area was extensive, with Army camps at Aldershot, Ash Vale, Bordon, Bramshott, Church Crookham, Deepcut, Ewshot, Guildford, Longmoor, Minley, Mytchett, Pirbright, Sandhurst, Thursley, Winchester and Witley, as well as the RAF at Odiham and Dunsfold, the Royal Aircraft Establishment, Farnborough and what was later to become the National Gas Turbine Establishment at Pyestock.

Company records show that, throughout its history, in times of peace and war, A&D has provided bus and coach services which routinely carried regular and National Service troops. Many local and long-distance stage-carriage bus services were developed to meet the needs of the Army, with numerous routes specifically operated from towns to army camps. When required there were special express coach services for military personnel to travel to and from London. One such service operated at 17.30 hours on Friday afternoons from Bordon Camp. This was a feeder service for the 17.30 'London' from Farnham, with the driver hurrying along to catch up with the 'London' to make the connection at Bagshot. At midnight on the following Sunday a convoy of Special Military Personnel Express Services departed from Victoria to destinations a) Bordon Camp, b) Southwood Camp, Cove and Crookham, and c) Blackdown and Deepcut camps. Tickets were purchased during the journey from a travelling conductor who alternated between the various coaches at specific stops between Victoria and Chiswick.

The bus provided soldiers with the means to travel from the camp, either into town — to visit the cinema, the local pub or meet girlfriends — or to (or from) the railway station when going on (or returning from) leave. It was an inspiration to watch A&D drivers and conductors controlling drunks and averting confrontation on such services, and they became very adept with their inter-personal skills. During times of conflict troops were transported by bus to the railway station or other destinations for embarkation to distant shores, while in peacetime specialist services were provided for routine troop movements. To thousands of soldiers from both the British Isles and overseas, the sight of a green-and-cream A&D bus, together with its friendly crew, represented at best the start of furlough and at worst a return to barracks or leaving for war. So, like us locals, many of the soldiers based in the area came to appreciate A&D, and, since the intake of soldiers arrived from all over the UK and abroad, A&D became well-known both at home and overseas.

When faced with war in 1939, A&D responded, as it had at the start of World War 1, by providing buses both for war service and for special workings to transport troops. During 1940 — probably the bleakest period of the war for the British nation, when the Army had

been forced to abandon vast numbers of vehicles during the evacuation of France — large numbers of civilian vehicles were requisitioned for military service. The records show that A&D had 49 vehicles requisitioned — virtually all of the older Dennis E and EV vehicles, plus others awaiting disposal, together with Dennis Lancet Is and the oldest Lancet IIs. Only nine Lancet IIs and three Lancet Is were returned at the end of hostilities. A&D buses would also disappear from local services when necessary to support the war, typically for a few days but sometimes for as much as a week. This was the result of widespread short-term commandeering of buses by the Army as part of Army Service troop movements or in response to demands by the Aldershot or Southern Command.

Aldershot was also the headquarters of the Canadian Army Overseas and, together with the surrounding camps at Bordon, Bramshott, Witley and RAF Odiham, was the main centre for Canadian troops arriving in the UK. For most of the war there were more Canadian than British troops in the Aldershot area, and we recall as children our frequent requests made to Canadian soldiers of 'Got any gum, chum?', to which they usually responded with gum or chocolate; they also organised parties for children at the various camps. It was in support of the Canadian Army that possibly one of the largest A&D troop movements was made during the war when, in 1943, a total of 32 buses were provided to transport 1,000 Canadian soldiers to Salisbury.

The records also show that, in anticipation of heavy casualties from the bombing of major towns in Southern England, plans were in place before commencement of the war for the conversion of 45 A&D Dennis Lancet I coaches and single-deck buses into emergency ambulances, with volunteer drivers. Within days of declaration of war the vehicles had been stripped, re-fitted to carry 10 stretchers and painted grey to reduce visibility to enemy aircraft. Fortunately none of these ambulances was lost to enemy action, and, as the liberation of Europe progressed and the threat of intensive air raids receded, the vehicles were gradually released and started to reappear in A&D service, although it was to be some time before they reverted to A&D livery.

The evacuated children (mainly from London) who had arrived on special trains at railway stations in the A&D operating area — notably Farncombe — in September 1939 would have found A&D buses with friendly crews waiting to take them to the safety of villages in the local area. Many of these evacuees joined local children in their schooling.

Military bands have always been popular, and from the 1920s A&D regularly provided coaches to transport the bandsmen and their instruments on tours or to concerts in cities, towns and seaside resorts. In the early 1930s the extensive range of musical instruments had been placed on the roof and carried using a long steel roof rack. However, the introduction in the mid-1930s of the 'bandbox', with the metal sidewalls, strengthened roof, the four chromium-plated hinged steps in the nearside rear panel and the two-rung ladder extending above, provided both improved access and improved security. The long bandbox was discontinued on all new coaches from 1938, but the shortened form, used as either a bandbox or luggage space, together with steps and ladder, became a feature on the majority of Strachans-bodied A&D single-deck buses until the late 1940s. A&D continued regularly to transport military bands postwar, although with the greater availability of army lorries for transportation of the instruments there was no need for specially adapted buses. Although the shortened bandbox was discontinued on all new single-deck buses from 1949, it was not removed from most of the existing vehicles until late in their

At the outbreak of World War 2, 45 of the company's buses, including many of the older Dennis Lancets, were converted into ambulances. A grey-painted, 1936-vintage Lancet is seen at Park Prewett Hospital, near Basingstoke, where wounded service personnel were transported, mainly from Southampton Docks. Unlike the buses requisitioned by the Army, all the Lancets used as ambulances returned to normal service after the war.
Peter Trevaskis collection

Dennis Lancet II BOT 288, introduced late in 1936, was the first of a new breed of 94 similar buses to be purchased over the next five years. They carried the revised, more stylish radiator design, flared skirt panels, integral cab and seated 32 passengers in rear-entrance bodywork by either Strachans or Dennis. The first 10 were fitted with large 'band boxes' surmounted by a steel-railed rack — ideal for carrying military-band instruments in safety. Sadly BOT 288, requisitioned for military service in 1940, was never returned to its original owner. *Peter Holmes collection*

Captured in wartime guise, with headlamp masks, white mudguard edging and no fleetname, DHO 273 was the first of the all-Dennis Lancet IIs delivered in 1939. With windscreen and side windows open, the bus is seen leaving Reading on a hot summer's day, probably in 1943. Behind is a Thames Valley Leyland Tiger TS8, its roof brackets an indication that it was once used regularly on Reading–London services. *Gerry Bixley collection*

Dennis Lancet II 832 (DHO 295) has just arrived in Barrack Road, Aldershot, from Farnborough in the early 1950s. Although regular timetabled journeys on service 3 (Aldershot–Farnborough Station) had ceased in September 1942, the number was retained for duplicate workings. The route traversed Queen's Avenue, which was lined by numerous barracks as well as central facilities such as the Garrison Headquarters. This batch of Lancets had their roof-mounted luggage racks removed in 1949/50 and were withdrawn in 1953/4. *Martin Brown*

▲ In Blackdown Camp, served by A&D buses since World War 1, Dennis Loline III 452 (452 EOT) stands at the terminus of the long (95min) journey on service 34A from Guildford in April 1969. The circuitous route home would be via Frimley Green, Camberley, Bagshot, Lightwater, Knaphill, Woking, Mayford and Stoke. *Mike Stephens*

After World War 2 the NAAFI built a number of new clubs in the main military centres to provide facilities for off-duty servicemen (and, in some places, rooms for their visiting parents!). The Aldershot NAAFI Club forms the backdrop for rebodied Guy Arab II 888 (EOT 25) as it leans away from the roundabout at the junction of the High Street and Station Road on 30 July 1960. The combination of 8ft-wide body on a 7ft 6in chassis tended to produce an alarming tilting effect when cornering at speed. *Tony Wright*

Service 68 had a chequered life. Essentially an express service to carry troops from the outlying Guillemont Barracks, near Cove, to Farnborough and Aldershot stations, it absorbed a similar service from Southwood Barracks and became very sparse before finally ceasing at the end of 1968. This view of AEC Reliance 316 (SOU 424) at the Guillemont terminus was recorded on 25 August 1967. *Mike Stephens*

lives. To this day, we remain disappointed that we never had the opportunity to pull out the hinged steps and clamber up over the ladder to the bandbox; indeed, during our 'glory days' we never saw the bandbox used.

During the Fifties and Sixties soldiers from the various Guards regiments based in Aldershot and Pirbright were routinely carried to Wellington Barracks in London to perform guard duties at Buckingham Palace, where they participated in the famous 'Changing of the Guard' ceremony. The sight of guardsmen seated on the coaches with their brightly coloured red uniforms dancing on hangers suspended from the luggage racks was a treat! With the advent of improved military transport and greater use of the railway — and, latterly, aircraft, used to deploy troops to distant shores — the need for A&D coaches reduced.

At the Farnborough Air Show held in September 1962, some 19 A&D buses are seen lined up in Alexandra Road awaiting the surge of patrons at the end of the display. Dennis Lance K3s and K4s predominate. *Peter Trevaskis*

8. Farnborough Air Show

The authors' earliest memories of the annual Farnborough Air Show are still vivid today after 50 years. This is probably because of two things. First, it was (and, indeed, still is) a huge international event bringing new, noisy aircraft to the skies above a relatively small town on the Hampshire/Surrey border. Secondly, the influx of thousands of visitors, many of whom arrived by car, brought chaos to traffic; much to the annoyance of local residents, the normal bus timetable was disrupted considerably, with buses running up to an hour late. However, to a couple of young enthusiasts, clambering on the temporary steel barriers placed at the pavement edge to funnel the queues, the sight of a long line of assorted buses and coaches in side streets not normally graced by buses at all was an exciting prospect. During the 1950s and 1960s it was common to see a row of Guy Arabs, Dennis Lance K3s and K4s, Falcons, Lancets and coaches stretching along Church Road and Guildford Road. Inspectors, calling out the departure of the next full bus, were assigned to the streets as well.

A&D had the annual contract to carry visitors to and from the local stations of North Camp and Aldershot on a regular shuttle service; the majority used the latter station. Convoys of buses travelled the two miles between the Air Show and Aldershot for much of the day. Public days were always at the weekend after the week of displays for the commercial world. Endless aircraft rehearsals for six weeks or so before the actual Air Show meant that to local people the final displays were less exciting than they were to the fresh eyes and ears of visitors! However, there were still some spectacular, memorable moments, particularly in September 1949, when the huge Brabazon airliner first came into view over the trees behind the garden in Cove. This giant of the skies made an impression on many local people, such that, as stated earlier, the next batch of larger single-deckers delivered to A&D were nicknamed 'Brabs'; to this day, the 12 Dennis Lancet J10s which joined the fleet in 1950 are referred to by this name.

What never occurred to us was the massive task of organising

The September 1955 Air Show sees Dennis Lance II 754 (CCG 351) at the head of the line in Reading Road, Farnborough, ready to take returning passengers to Aldershot station. At this time the main railway line through Farnborough was not electrified, so Aldershot was much better-suited to dealing with large numbers of additional passengers. *David Sharwood*

The Air Display lull. Having delivered their many passengers, mostly off trains from Aldershot station, operating staff from all depots rest in the gardens near the old Farnborough Town Hall on 8 September 1962. When the crowds emerge from the show the buses will load up in adjacent Reading Road (36 seconds were allowed!) for the return runs. *Peter Trevaskis*

the special routes over the two public days. A 'Tracco' Departmental Memorandum of 1951 shows how the company planned for the onset of the crowds visiting the Air Show by train. 'Five single-decked buses will be allocated to operate the special services between North Camp Station and Church Road, Farnborough, on both days. To provide additional vehicles at short notice, intimation to our Inspector at Church Road Park will receive immediate attention.' In the same year there was an allocation of '10 double-decked and 25 single-decked vehicles to operate between Aldershot Town Station and Church Road, Farnborough'.

It is interesting to note that the five single-deckers mentioned were operated as duplicate buses from Woking on route 44 (Woking–Aldershot) between 09.15 and 11.15, ready for duties at North Camp station. For the Aldershot Station shuttle run on Saturday 15 September 1951 buses were 'borrowed' from several depots: eight double-deckers and 17 single-deckers came from nearby Aldershot, one double-decker and four single-deckers from Guildford and one double-decker and four single-deckers from Hindhead. To meet the anticipated greater demand on the following day, 14 double-deckers and 10 single-deckers came from the local depot, with four double-deckers and five single-deckers travelling from Guildford and two double-deckers and five single-deckers from Hindhead. On that weekend there were 11 special trains each day terminating at Aldershot. Spectators had to be in their places by 15.00, when the air display started. When the massive crowd began to leave the airfield between 17.00 and 18.00, the shuttle services recommenced. It was a hectic time, with the important task of conveying hundreds of families to the waiting trains.

Company variation orders were in force as well because of the traffic conditions. The A&D Traffic Manager had informed drivers and conductors that 'the ordinary services 3B, 3D and 41 will be re-routed' to avoid the A325 main road and entrances to the airfield, where queues of cars congested the area. Routes 3B and 3D were local hourly single-decker services serving new estates in Cove, on the western outskirts of Farnborough, about five miles from Aldershot. These routes were operated frequently by Lancets — J3s and J10s — the timings being far less reliable during the Show week. The small diversion away from part of the A325 helped, but traffic volumes hindered progress at peak times. In the 1950s route 41, from Farnborough station to Farnham, was likely to be operated by one of the Leyland TD7s. With only one trip each way for commuters, the delays did not affect so many people. As well as these, the normal

On a sunny September evening in 1960 one of Guildford depot's Dennis Lancet J10s has been drafted in to assist in returning Air Show patrons from Farnborough to North Camp station. They have just disembarked and are making their way to the station, where the wide platforms, originally designed to handle large troop movements, are ideal for dealing with the special trains to and from the Midlands via Reading. The North Camp shuttle service, unlike that to Aldershot station, was operated entirely with single-deckers. *Peter Trevaskis*

After the Air Show, pre-booked passengers assemble to board coaches in Alexandra Road, Farnborough, on 12 September 1959. The first London-bound coach, Strachans-bodied AEC Reliance 262 (MOR 593), is almost full, but there are others waiting to be filled behind. *Peter Trevaskis*

A hectic scene in Guildford Road, Farnborough, after the Air Show on 12 September 1959. The 24-seat Dennis Falcon P3, 153 (GOU 853), is not the most suitable vehicle for dealing with large numbers, which shows how stretched the company was in coping with the demand. *Peter Trevaskis*

▲ routes to Camberley (1, 2 and 3C) and the Farnborough locals (3A and 71) were affected and suffered from poor timing. We have clear memories of joining the traditional Sunday-evening gathering around a local landmark — the Clockhouse in Farnborough — to watch the homeward chaos. Together with local residents we would sit on the raised kerb at the foot of the building and stare in amazement at the wide variety of buses, coaches, vans and cars crawling home after the show. Even if it was wet, we carried on with this silent tradition. This was the age of liberation as more people began to own a car. One thing which remains in our minds is the picture of very wet or very warm Air Show weeks — the week never seemed to enjoy a normal, balanced weather pattern! Whatever the weather, however, most of the aerobatic displays — apart, perhaps, from the high-flying Red Arrow formations — would continue. Of course, there were problems: one year we saw a French aircraft fly too low over the edge of the airfield when landing and crash on the Mess and famous 'Black Sheds'. Regrettably there were a number of fatalities, and we recollect the ensuing traffic hold-ups and diversions, which caused even greater congestion all around the area.

Two weeks before the 1951 Air Show the A&D Traffic Manager at Aldershot wrote: 'Very large crowds are expected … and in the event of any instruction being given to Drivers by the Police with a view to easing any temporary congestion which may occur, such instructions are to be carried out and every effort made to co-operate with a view to ensuring a smooth flow of vehicular traffic'. In most cases buses travelled from Guildford, Woking or Hindhead as duplicates to normal services to Aldershot before travelling 'dead' to the Air Show to take up their special duties; Alton depot appears not to have participated in this large-scale operation. The Traffic Manager's predictions were correct — there were vast crowds. For the privilege of travelling on these special non-stop shuttle services, the fare was 6d single and 1/- return.

In 1952 the number of spectators was even greater, as the popularity of the air displays grew in response to the tremendous developments in aviation in the early-postwar period. Much the same arrangements were made by A&D, although the expectation of increased traffic and experience gained from the demand in the previous year is obvious from the allocation of vehicles. There were still five buses for the North Camp shuttle run, but 45 buses on Saturday 6 September and 50 buses on Sunday 7 September booked to operate the trips to and from Aldershot.

By 1960 the number of 'public' days had increased to three with the inclusion of Fridays as part of a long weekend of viewing the show and displays. With no prior knowledge as to numbers, the company deployed eight double-deckers and 12 single-deckers from Aldershot depot to operate the Friday shuttles on 9 September. In addition to this, over the remainder of the weekend 45 vehicles were used on both days, with an interesting development of the use of 38 double-deckers on Sunday 11 September, drawn from Aldershot (19), Alresford (1), Winchester (1), Guildford (10), Hindhead (3) and Woking (4).

As well as being faced with moving passengers and buses, the company had to ensure that it had sufficient staff in the correct place for each Show day. It is fascinating to read the contemporary records for 1961, which provide an insight as to how crews were positioned for the Air Show specials. Instructions relating to the two double-deckers borrowed on Saturday 9 September from Hindhead depot were that 'at night, these vehicles will be garaged at Aldershot, the crews returning as passengers to Hindhead'. As for the five double-deckers borrowed the same day from Woking depot, 'At night, four of these vehicles will be garaged at Aldershot, the crews returning as passengers to Woking. The fifth double-decker will collect the four crews from Aldershot Garage, and return DEAD to Woking.' Similar arrangements were made for the vehicle

contribution from Guildford, although the single-deckers were returned. 'The two single-decker buses will return DEAD to Guildford on completion of Shuttle service. If released from Aldershot they will proceed direct to Guildford, otherwise if released from Farnborough, they will proceed via Services 35 and 39 to Dover Arms, Ash, thence via 20 route to Guildford.' By 1961 the fares had increased to 10d single and 1/6 return on the special journeys.

Farnborough International Air Show still flourishes today, although it is now a biennial July event, with local service buses providing transport links. However, following the introduction of the Blackwater Valley Road (A331) linking the M3 and A31, there is far less traffic chaos around the town on the public days.

Towards the end of A&D's separate existence, loading and unloading at Farnborough Town Hall for the Air Show seemed, for some reason, to go less smoothly than in earlier years. Dennis Loline III 525 (AAA 525C) and Loline 349 (SOU 457) typify these latter days. *Mike Stephens*

9. Garages and Support Services

Each of the three main towns served by A&D had its own garage situated in town. Often we enthusiasts would venture nearby in the hope of getting a glimpse into the yard and seeing something rare — a damaged Lancet, perhaps, or a withdrawn Guy — although our attempts were hindered by the combination of our small stature and the high fencing. At the time when we were growing up, the garage in Halimote Road, Aldershot —just a short walk from the bus station — was extended. During the 1960s the depot could accommodate 144 vehicles. Later, in 1968, there was a major refurbishment of the garage and adjacent Head Office. Guildford had a large garage, built in 1927 in Woodbridge Road, on the outskirts of town. This was extended in 1958 to include a new workshop, offices and stores. The roof span was considerable — about 120ft without pillars — and there was room for 91 vehicles under cover. Likewise, Woking garage was extended in 1952. All of these changes

reminded us of the growth of the bus industry and the expansion of these important towns on the Hampshire/Surrey border.

The main garage and Head Office at Aldershot had roots going back as far as 1915, when the site of a former brickworks was purchased. The land itself, by the junction of Halimote Road and Grosvenor Road, was quite steeply sloped; this allowed for a garage building, high enough for double-deckers, to be constructed with its roof just below the level of Grosvenor Road, but the workshop opened up on to that road, always being known affectionately as 'The Top Shop'. The sloping driveway leading to/from the garage site was known as Foden Road, after the fleet of Foden steam wagons which used to gather ready for their local journeys at the start of each day. There were many changes to the buildings as the company grew. In 1964 the Head Office building was modernised completely, and four years later there began a further improvement of the garage. Just before the

Entering Guildford garage for refuelling after operating the four-mile service from the village of Wood Street in June 1961, Dennis Loline 350 (SOU 458) was originally based at Aldershot and operated mainly on service 20 to Guildford. New in 1958, it was sold out of service in 1970. *Peter Trevaskis*

company finished in 1971, a new gyratory system was introduced whereby buses entered at the lower end (nearer the bus station) to refuel, before passing through a modern bus wash and parking up; all buses left from the upper end (nearer Grosvenor Road), using the original Foden Road. (Previously Foden Road had been used as both an entrance and an exit.) A reduced site remains in use today with A&D's successor, though the upper part, along Foden Road, has been redeveloped for housing.

The next-most-important garage was at Guildford, which unusually had two depots — one for A&D and one for London Transport. The earliest site for a garage in Guildford was in 1919, when a small building in Onslow Street was acquired by A&D. Until that time, about five buses had been garaged in Puttock's garage, off the High Street, but expansion of services meant that larger garage facilities were now necessary. Onslow Street garage housed 26 buses, but even that had become too small by 1927, when the Woodbridge site was developed. This huge corner site at the junction of two main roads seemed ideal,

making it easy for the company to deploy buses to all parts of the area. The garage was impressive, yet its original capacity of 55 buses was extended in 1958 to accommodate 36 more vehicles. In fact, this large garage site remained in use beyond A&D days, until 1985, when it was replaced by commercial premises.

Woking garage, a short walk from the town centre and railway station, was situated in Goldsworth Road. It was often fairly quiet, with a few single-deckers parked outside in the courtyard created in 1960. The original 1931 garage on the site accommodated 33 vehicles — mostly single-deckers, because of the restrictions on the use of double-deckers caused by numerous railway bridges around Woking; where double-deckers could be used, these were always of the lowbridge type. By 1953 the garage had been extended to house 43 buses, and seven years later the front by the roadside was redesigned to incorporate a bus stop and a parking area for buses on layover. The garage remained in use after the demise of A&D, until 1982.

In addition to the three main garages were two others, at Alton and Hindhead. Opened in 1931 with capacity for 45 buses,

Just off of the A3 London Road, Hindhead garage, seen here in 1945, was opened in June 1931 to replace the old garage in Clay Hill, Haslemere, and could accommodate 45 vehicles under cover. The yard at the rear was used to store delicensed buses awaiting disposal, and some of the petrol-engined Tilling-Stevens single-deckers were kept here for the duration of World War 2. The approach road, where buses waiting to go into service were lined up, was often used to carry out 'under the bonnet' adjustments, before the workshop and inspection pits were installed in the mid-1960s. *The Omnibus Society*

Alton depot in June 1966. Dennis Falcon P5 281 (POR 427) has worked across from Haslemere as a 13 via Kingsley, and its blinds are now set for the return journey by the 13A routeing through Oakhanger. *Philip Wallis*

Hindhead garage was situated on the main A3 trunk road. Alton depot was tucked away down a side road called Amery Street. By far the company's smallest garage, it was an important base for the rural routes around the town and in 1952 was expanded from the original garage built in 1932 with capacity for six buses. It often played host to a Wilts & Dorset double-decker or a Southdown single-decker, being an outstation for the former's Basingstoke service and for the latter company's Leylands operated on country route 38 between Alton and Portsmouth following closure of the Meon Valley railway line in 1955.

Various outstations, such as those at Alresford, Egham, Elstead, Ewhurst and Odiham, were still in use when we were young enthusiasts. In the mid-Sixties the introduction of more one-man-operated services saw the end of Ewhurst, because buses could not safely be shunted unassisted by a lone driver. Surprisingly, all the other outstations outlived A&D, showing how important

a role they played in the provision of the area's bus services.

As well as the depots and outstations, the company needed the main bus stations at Aldershot and Guildford and a whole range of enquiry and booking offices for its services. As well as these designated A&D buildings, there were smaller retailers like Drews, the stationer's at Farnborough Clockhouse, where we have fond memories of getting coach tickets for London or a summer excursion from Miss Noyse, who would always have time for a chat about the latest news or change in the weather. Other similar outlets were dotted throughout the network and provided local communities with the opportunity to purchase tickets in advance — essential for longer-distance travel in the Fifties and Sixties. Parcels could be sent by bus as well, and the same retailers would take in any goods which had to connect with a certain bus along the route passing by. Some through tickets for passengers could be bought from the bus conductor: a ticket purchased on the Guildford–Horsham bus, for example,

This nearside view of Bristol RELL6G 618 (YHO 618J) shows clearly the dual-door configuration of its Marshall 'standee' body. Standing in the approach road to Hindhead garage in November 1972, the bus still carries the A&D livery and fleetname, albeit with a red Alder Valley fleet-number plate.
Brian Oxborough

Ewhurst outstation was situated within the premises of a small market garden in Gadbridge Lane, Ewhurst. The bus stationed there spent most of its working day on service 33 (Guildford–Horsham), and its positioning journeys were on service 23 (Guildford–Ewhurst). When this picture was taken, in June 1960, the occupant was 43-seat AEC Reliance 329 (SOU 437). The outstation closed in March 1968, by which time one-man operation had become widespread and the absence of a conductor to assist reversing in this tight location was leading to problems. *David Sharwood*

In the early days the outstation at Alresford had been in a public-house yard, but the best-remembered location was this converted barn on the western outskirts of the town, which accommodated a double-decker used on service 14 (Aldershot–Winchester); at the time of this June 1965 photograph the occupant was Dennis Loline 353 (SOU 461). Use of this building continued into Alder Valley days. *Peter Trevaskis*

would permit its holder to travel beyond A&D territory on Southdown buses to Worthing.

Other support services included the use of redundant buses as tree-loppers. One which the authors particularly recall (although not the first) was a Guy Arab double-decker converted to open-top and painted all-over dark green; as, during the 'glory days' the company never used open-top buses on its services, this was a rare vehicle to capture on film. Later A&D built up a retired Dennis Falcon to become a handy tree-lopper for the wooded routes. Meanwhile small Morris service vans would scurry about the place with Inspectors, paperwork for new timetables at bus stops and, no doubt, many other important aspects of the daily routine. Like the buses, these vans were given fleet numbers and painted green.

A line-up at Aldershot bus station, on 1 July 1951, of buses employed on long trunk services. On the left, 696 (BOT 290), one of the first oil-engined Dennis Lancet IIs dating from 1937 (and destined to be withdrawn within three months) is on service 44 to Woking. No 781 (COR 177) was on service 6 to Petersfield and Steep. The unique Dennis Dominant, 174 (HOU 900), has yet to change its blinds for the next 19 service to Midhurst (or maybe even on further, to Bognor Regis), while, on the right, Dennis Lance K3 129 (GOU 829) of Alresford outstation awaits departure on service 14 to Winchester. *David Sharwood*

The company's timetables in 1965 showed a coloured view of Aldershot bus station, after the through platforms had been abolished and end-loading bays substituted the previous year.

▲ A view of Aldershot bus station, taken in the early 1960s from the roof of Gale & Polden's printing works, showing the earlier (1933) bays on the left and the through platforms added in 1950 on the right. *Tony Wright collection*

Aldershot bus station opened on 15 January 1934, but several services still had to use local streets as their terminus, and on 20 March 1950 an extension was opened to accommodate some of these. A month later, on 22 April, an 8 service to Fleet stands at one of the new platforms; the information board would have been sign-written in the company's own premises. CCG 348 was one of the 1937 Dennis Lance IIs rebodied by East Lancs between 1944 and 1948. Later in 1950, fleet numbers started to be applied to the company's vehicles; CCG 348 became 751 and survived until 1958. *David Sharwood*

Guildford's Farnham Road bus station opened on 11 May 1950 and was managed by A&D on behalf of Guildford Borough Council. This bird's-eye view from the tower of St Nicolas' church was recorded in the late 1960s. In addition to the A&D vehicles visible, at the bottom left can be seen a Thames Valley Bristol LS bound for Bracknell and Reading on service 75, operated jointly with A&D. At the rear of the middle platform is an RF of London Transport's Country Area; behind that, on the stand adjacent to the enquiry office, is a Bedford of Safeguard Coaches. *Peter Sherwood*

▲ Tree-cutting was an essential activity, and not only on rural routes. In November 1964 Guy Arab 31 (EOR 374), cut down in 1958 from a 'utility' bus delivered in 1945, provides employment to staff whose summer duty as crews for excursions and tours had been curtailed by the short winter days. This scene was recorded in Farnborough Park, on the route of service 71B (North Camp–Hawley Estates).
Peter Trevaskis

▲ New in 1956, Dennis Falcon P5 275 (POR 421) originally carried a 30-seat forward-entrance Strachans body. When withdrawn in 1967 it was rebuilt as a tree-cutter to replace the ageing Guy Arab and was numbered 46 in the A&D service fleet, in which it survived into Alder Valley days. The other seven buses of its batch were sold to Isle of Man Road Services, one of which, 282 (POR 428), has since returned to Hampshire and is undergoing restoration. *Les Smith collection*

In 1961 Dennis Lancet bus 114 (GOU 814) was cut down to produce a towing lorry. This was numbered 38 and always ran on trade plates 141 AA. It is seen here at the rear of Hindhead depot.
Les Smith

Since 1994 the Aldershot & District Bus Interest Group (ADBIG) has held several Running Days, and has also contributed vehicles to numerous bus rallies across the South of England. Preserved but not yet in running condition, Dennis Lancet J3 express coach 980 (GAA 616) was a static exhibit at the 1995 ADBIG Running Day at Guildford. Delivered in 1948, the 15 coaches of this type were used on the Farnham–London service for five years; subsequently they could be seen on excursions and 'Coastals'. *Les Smith*

10. Reliving the Glory Days

During our 'glory days' period, from our earliest recollections during World War 2, we witnessed significant advances in the design of A&D buses and coaches. Fortunately, through the preservation of a number of former A&D Dennis and AEC single-deck buses and coaches and Dennis double-deck buses, we are able to recapture the contribution made by A&D to our transport heritage from the postwar era to the demise of the company in 1971. As a living museum, these vehicles also represent an important part of our local history and industrial archæology, enabling us to relive those special moments of our formative years and providing the young with the opportunity to sample the experience of travel by bus in the 1940s, '50s and '60s.

Unfortunately no A&D buses or coaches fitted with petrol engines survive from our 'glory days' period, so we need to await the renovation of the recently secured 1920s Dennis E chassis for the opportunity to experience travel in such a vehicle.

We are, however, encouraged at the prospect of travelling on examples of a Dennis Lancet J3 coach and single-deck bus when renovation is completed. We look forward to achieving boyhood ambitions of climbing those retractable steps at the rear of the Strachans bus bodywork and gaining access to that roof-mounted bandbox!

The oldest operational single-deck bus in the preserved A&D fleet is provided by the Dennis Lancet J10, the 'Brab'. We consider it a real treat to rediscover the performance of the Dennis O6 engine and five-speed gearbox in what was to prove the last and largest half-cab single-deck type operated by the company. With five-speed overdrive gearbox the 'Brab' can still achieve speeds in excess of 50mph, which we considered very fast in the halcyon days of our youth. Moreover, it is reassuring to note that, just as we experienced back in the 1950s, if not closed properly the rear door can still gradually slide open when the vehicle is in motion! The prospect of travelling on the Dennis

Lancet J10C coach following completion of renovation will remind us of earlier excursions to the seaside and give us the chance to re-evaluate, with the benefit of hindsight, the combination of Strachans' full-fronted body styling and A&D's traditional rear entrance.

The only remaining Dennis Falcon P5 'conker box' is also undergoing renovation, and we await the opportunity to reassess the levels of the engine noise permeating the saloon. This vehicle is of particular historical importance, being both the last Falcon P5 produced by Dennis and, of greater significance locally, the last Dennis single-deck bus supplied to A&D. Although it may not be as cute as the smaller Dennis Ace, the Falcon P5 is interesting, because, with the driver seated in the saloon, in close proximity to the passengers, it maintains the intimacy established between driver and passengers on 'deep rural' routes.

All of the preserved A&D Dennis single-deckers, in their various stages of restoration, permit us to observe how buses with the engine mounted vertically at the front of the chassis were constructed until the mid-1950s: with the exception of the Falcon P5, which is fitted with an all-metal, front-entrance body, the preserved Strachans-bodied single-deckers all exhibit the wooden-frame construction, overlaid with metal panels, once employed by bodybuilders.

We can appreciate the transition from traditional pre-1950s bus construction to the concept of the underfloor horizontally-mounted engine, together with state-of-the-art single-deck body design at the time, through two examples of the AEC Reliance. One is a 1954 MU3RV type, initially operated as a coach with a Strachans Everest body but re-entering service in 1967 with a new BET-style MCW bus body, while the other is a 1960 2MU3RV type with original Weymann BET-design bus body. Comparison with the earlier, Strachans-bodied single-deck buses shows how Weymann introduced a more open and airy saloon, with improved visibility through the windows. When these buses

Weymann-bodied AEC Reliance 370 (XHO 370) is seen at Cranleigh while taking part in the ADBIG members' Autumn Tour on 5 October 2002. New to A&D in 1960, it was withdrawn by Alder Valley in 1975, after which it saw service as a mobile mission church, latterly in Northern Ireland, from where it was resurrected for preservation in 1996. The notice on the entrance had been altered to read 'Please <u>Pray</u> as you Enter'! No 370 now takes part regularly in running days, rallies and tours etc, having been restored to the later dark-green livery style.
Tony Wright

AEC Reliance 543 (MOR 581) entered service with A&D as 250 in 1954 with a 41-seat, centre-entrance Strachans Everest coach body. Early in 1967 it was fitted with new 40-seat Metro-Cammell bus bodywork similar in style to that on other Reliances in the fleet. Now preserved in this form and carrying the earlier livery style, it is shown taking part in the Mid-Hants Railway Running Day at Alton station on 14 July 2002. *Tony Wright*

take to the road, a surprising number of passengers remark upon the contemporary body styling, expressing their belief that the Reliance is a relatively modern bus. However, the lack of power and speed when compared with our perception of the performance in the late 1950s and 1960s confirms to us that the Reliance certainly is *not* a modern vehicle.

It is refreshing to revisit the hazards of travelling on lowbridge double-deckers with sunken gangway in the upper saloon, made possible by the preserved Dennis Lance K3 and K4 vehicles. The sunken gangway continues to be a novelty to many passengers. We remember to lower our heads as we leave our seats along the offside of the lower saloon, and struggle to alight from the bench seats in the upper saloon, as we had done so many years earlier. Upstairs, demonstrations of the disturbance caused to fellow passengers as the passenger furthest from the gangway attempts to leave his/her seat — especially a bench seat for three or four — still cause amusement. The practices we

employed, of climbing over fellow passengers or persuading them to move into the gangway, have not changed, and utter chaos still ensues in the upper saloon when several passengers seated in different rows attempt to alight at the same destination. However, it was not so amusing in the past, when laden with heavy bags of shopping or satchels full of homework.

The Dennis Loline and the three operational Loline III double-decker buses provide the opportunity to experience a more modern approach to bus operation, with higher passenger-carrying capacity and a more passenger-friendly environment than on earlier double-deckers. Fitted with the more powerful Gardner 6LW engine, the Lolines compare favourably in terms of performance (and ride) with the K3 and K4 Lances, fitted with Dennis O6 and Gardner 5LW engines respectively. Observing the driver from the saloon, we can see the physical exertion necessary to drive the older vehicles, especially when steering and changing gear with the crash-type gearboxes. Isolated in his cab, the driver

Immaculate East Lancs-bodied Dennis Lance K4 220 (LOU 48)
is captured in Horsell High Street, nearing the Cricketers Inn, on
a 28B journey while taking part in the ADBIG Golden Jubilee
Running Day on 2 June 2002. No fewer than nine preserved
'Tracco' buses took part in this very successful event. Like the
earlier K3, 220 is the sole survivor of its type. New in 1954,
it was withdrawn from service in 1965. *Tony Wright*

is cold in winter, with no heater
and with cold draughts passing up
through the floor, and very hot in
summer, when, even with the
windscreen and side windows
open, there is insufficient airflow
for adequate ventilation. When it
rains he strains to see through the
band of clear vision left on the
windscreen by the small wiper
blade and struggles to clear
condensation with his
handkerchief. Things are little
better in the saloon, which is cold
in winter, thanks to the inefficiency
of the heaters, and stifling hot in
summer. Despite these
discomforts, the conversations
between conductor and passengers,
together with the general chatter
between passengers, are all very
reminiscent of the community
spirit which bus travel used to
engender during the 'glory days'.

The only significant difference
in the appearance of the double-
deckers in preservation when
compared with their working
lives with A&D is the limited
application of external advertising.
In A&D days advertisements were
routinely displayed, and we
followed with great interest the
changes in the national and local
brands featured. Whilst the
absence of such advertisements
represents a lack of authenticity,
we respect the owners' reasons for
their omission. After all, without
the commitment and dedication
of the small number of A&D
preservationists, we would not
be able to relive part of A&D's
'glory days'.

21 April 1996 saw the first ADBIG Running Day to be held in Woking. On this occasion the A&D vehicles were assisted by ex-London Country buses. Dennis Loline 357 (SOU 465), with a 68-seat East Lancs body, is pictured opposite the Cricketers Inn at Horsell, ready to return to Woking on a 28B service. This was the last A&D type to have a rear entrance, albeit with a sliding door. *Tony Wright*

Restored by the Aldershot & District Omnibuses Rescue & Restoration Society (ADORRS), Weymann-bodied Dennis Loline III 488 (488 KOT) of 1964 made its debut at the Golden Jubilee Running Day and is seen — suitably adorned with Jubilee logos — at St John's, Woking, on 2 June 2002. Following restoration it has become the only Loline to be equipped with a wheelchair ramp and the fittings to allow two wheelchair-bound passengers to be carried in the lower saloon. *Les Smith*

On the Golden Jubilee Running Day at Woking on 2 June 2002, Loline 357 (SOU 465) and two Weymann-bodied Loline IIIs — 506 (AAA 506C) and 503 (AAA 503C) — rest at the end of a busy day, on which over 90 departures were scheduled on nostalgic local routes in the area. An added touch of authenticity is provided by 357's carrying period advertisements for local businesses on the front and side panels between the decks. *Tony Wright*

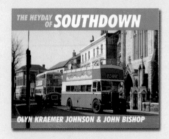